EAT.SLEEP.KAYAK .REPEAT

GRACE ALSANCAK-HAY

EAT.SLEEP.KAYAK.REPEAT

ISBN: 9798594156593

DEDICATION

To family, friends and all those incredible people who came to our aid while completing this challenge.

We couldn't have done it without any of you.

And for that I will be eternally grateful.

Thank you

x

CONTENTS

INTRODUCTION

Hello, thank you for picking up my book. If you were searching for it then well done, here it is, round of applause to you, you have completed your challenge. If you have picked it up by mistake, well I hope you enjoy it.

In the following pages I will give you a true no holds barred account of my time spent Kayaking the fourth longest river in the world; the Mississippi, in the summer of 2014.

So, a bit more about me then…at the time of starting this book I am 22, studying part time for a master's degree in Sports Coaching, and working as a diving coach for two local diving clubs. I was born in the town of Elland in West Yorkshire and have lived there ever since. In my spare time I take part in numerous sports and amateur dramatics.

Am I a professional Kayaker? No! Am I an experienced Kayaker? No! Have I ever even been in a Kayak? Yes! (on school trips and such) So I'm not quite as mad as you may think, but like everyone else I'm going to guess you are thinking, 'Grace, why did you decide to do this then?' Well, I will give you the detailed answer later but for now it's quite simple, because I could, and I believe when you are given an amazing opportunity like this there can only ever be one answer and that is 'bring it on'

So, if you are still reading it means I must be doing something right to keep you interested, so I will stop rambling now and get on with my story, it all started back in the May of 2012…

PART 1:
HALIFAX, WEST YORKSHIRE TO LAKE ITASCA AND THE SOURCE OF THE MISSISSIPPI RIVER

"If someone offers you an amazing opportunity and you're not sure you can do it, say yes – then learn how to do it later" Richard Branson

CHAPTER 1
LET'S START AT THE VERY BEGINNING

So how did this all begin? Well, here is the true and detailed story. I say true as I received unfounded criticism from many people before setting out on this adventure as they all seemed to believe it came about as just a crazy idea that I woke up with one morning. This couldn't be further from the truth.

People labelled Ken (my paddle partner) and myself as mad, reckless, selfish, or stupid, thought we didn't have a clue what we were doing and were putting our lives and others in danger. The list goes on and on. The assumption made by people was that Ken and I hadn't looked into the whole idea properly. Quick to judge our ideas people believed we had just decided to book flights to the States and jump on a boat down the 4th longest river in the world without any prior planning. Again, completely unfounded.

A good place to start would be to explain the relationship between Ken Robertshaw, and I. Ken (aged 58), and I (22) may seem a bit of a bizarre adventuring partnership, but before this challenge we had in fact know each other for a good-few-years and each classed the other as a good, trusted friend.

Back in 2009 I was selected by the Rotary Club of Elland to take part in a programme called the 'Rotary Youth Leadership Award' or RYLA for short. Ken was the course leader, and this is where we first met. A few years later (2011) he made contact with me to invite me to take part in the first RYLA international exchange he was coordinating following me having been a standout awardee from my year. Of course, I jumped at the chance and took part in the exchange visiting Sweden and hosting my exchange partner Josephine back home in England.

During the course Ken was asking me about my diving (I was still training and competing as a platform and springboard diver at this point) and how it feels to throw yourself off something a few stories high. I told him the best way to find out would be to do it and if he wanted, I would teach him.

To cut a long story short, everyone on the exchange programme ended up challenging him to dive off the five-metre platform at our local pool. After teaching him the basics he managed to do it and raised a few hundred pounds for charity.

During this period of time Ken and I spent some time talking about upcoming adventures we both had planned. Soon after leaving Sweden I was to head out to Tanzania to climb Mount Kilimanjaro through a trip organised by my University. A few months after my return Ken was to drive a dog sled team across the Arctic regions of Northern Europe for charity. Talk soon turned to what each of our next adventures would be, and Ken explained to me how, after watching a TV programme in the early hours of the morning featuring a leaf's journey down the Mississippi River he had thought that Kayaking down that same river could be an interesting challenge. In fact, he had already started doing some research for it. I thought it sounded like a great idea and said if it ever comes to fruition let me know. That was the end of the conversation for a good year.

In May 2012 Ken was delivering a talk about his adventure driving the dog sledding team at a meeting of a local group that my parents were part of and which I had gate-crashed. I had only late last year talked to that group about my trip to climb Mount Kilimanjaro.

Going through his presentation he began talking about his kit,

"We had to carry all our own equipment on the sleds, we didn't have people to do it for us"

He emphasised the last few words and shot a cheeky grin across the room at me. I knew exactly what he was alluding to. When I climbed Kilimanjaro, we had guides and porters with us as part of the team. They would set up our tents for us and carry most of our heavy gear. This is common practice on accents of mountains as the locals are far more adept to the environment and the lack of oxygen available and can therefore carry heavier loads while moving a lot faster than their clients. (I will forever be thankful to my porter without who I would never have made it to the top, in fact I think I would still be trying to get up there now.)

I knew what Ken was wanting so I replied…

"Well, you were just pulled along by dogs, I had to do it all by myself"

and so, our healthy sparing began…

"I had to handle half-wild dogs"

"I had to cope with altitude sickness"

…on and on we went coming up with facts and achievements that would out do the other, all done with a good sense of humour of course. Whether they got fed up with us having this debate or they were genuinely interested I will never know, but the next voice we heard asked

"So how are you going to settle this?"

Ken looked at me and once again brought up the idea of kayaking the Mississippi River. I knew from the look on his face that he meant it and not being one to back down from an adventure I said, "Okay then let's do it" and so the Mississippi Challenge was formed.

While agreeing to do the challenge may have been a quick decision the planning and preparation time was anything but.

For the next year we spent time talking about and discussing the idea between ourselves and others. We contacted people who had done the trip before for advice and most importantly put forward our ideas to family. My parents thought I was mad at first as they knew so little about the river. Their reaction to the idea was very similar to that of when I told them about Kilimanjaro, laughter, but then on realising I was serious and had done my research, they became supportive. They know my determination levels are high and that if I set myself a challenge, I will complete it. After all I only learned to do the Rubik's cube because a friend said I wouldn't be able to do it.

Having discussed the idea at length with my parents they were all for me going ahead and having this amazing experience, of course they had their reservations for my safety etc. as did I, but unfortunately however hard you try nothing is 100% safe.

On December the 30th 2013, Ken and I were hunched over an endless pile of maps and information on various aspects of the Mississippi River. This was the day we officially decided the trip was going to happen after over a year of 'if's and maybe's and plenty of research. A website was being built and we launched a Facebook page to promote ourselves. It had over 100 'likes' in 24 hours. Well, that was it there was no going back now.

I hear you asking… why on earth would you need a map to navigate a river, surely you just point your boat downstream and off you go. Yes, in theory that is the case, however the Mississippi is near enough a highway in the US and it takes on a variety of different forms from a small stream, to a 13 mile wide lake, or from a fast-flowing waterway for container ships, to being home to an international shipping port.

We needed to know where we could and couldn't go, what channels to take when the river split off, where to cross the lakes, how long it was likely to take and perhaps most importantly where we would be able to pick up provisions and stay for the night. It certainly wasn't just a case of turning up and paddling off downstream.

We discovered there were 28 locks (a device used for lowering and raising boats between parts of the river that are at various levels) that we would have to go through along with a set of rapids, and that two particular sections of river (approximately 150 miles above and below Memphis) were away from any kind of civilisation whatsoever and it would therefore be impossible to stock up on provisions including water during these sections.

Thorough research allowed us to put a rough timeline together. According to online information the Mississippi River was 2350 miles long and taking into account the different speeds we would likely be able to hit on different sections of the river we approximated needing to cover between 20-60 miles a day. (At the start of our journey we would likely manage around 15 miles as we wouldn't be helped along by any form of flow due to the river being so shallow, however as we moved down river towards the industrial ports the river would be deeper and dredged for the big ships meaning we would be able to move faster and achieve more like 60 miles a day). Taking all this into account we set ourselves a target of 60 days to complete the journey.

Along with researching all this type of information, we had to look into flights, visas, kayaks and all manner of kit; after all we were self-organising this and had no tour company to help us out, there was a lot to do and given that we had set ourselves a start date of July 2014 we didn't have long.

Skipping forward to January 2014 and to our first 'training session'. We borrowed equipment from the local scout camp and hit the 'Calder and Hebble' canal for our first real taste of kayaking.

I must mention here that even after Ken's words "that's not going anywhere" while securing the Kayaks to his car we did almost lose one as we turned a corner. The driver whose windscreen was in the firing line did not seem impressed. Thankfully Ken spotted the problem and grabbed hold of the rogue kayak before it fully slipped off the roof. I made a note to self: while on the Mississippi no matter how certain Ken is that "it's not going anywhere" it may well do!

Anyone near the Copley section of the Calder Canal that morning would have been thoroughly entertained. For the life in me I could not paddle in a straight line and just constantly turned around in a circle meaning I was paddling backwards most of the time, which I actually seemed to be better at! I would be lying if I said this didn't worry me, I had visions of myself zig zagging or going backwards all the way down the Mississippi. Ken wasn't much better, and we were both howling with laughter as he struggled to get himself out of his Kayak. We vowed to ourselves that we would get better, after all we needed to.

Knowing we needed to improve our paddling skills we quickly enlisted the help of a friend, Pete Richardson. Pete is a qualified Kayaking instructor and I had first met him on RYLA in 2009. He had agreed to teach me and Ken all he knew about paddling and more importantly some safety skills for if we got into difficulty on the river. This was brilliant, however Pete lived in Devon.

So, one evening in the February of 2014 Ken picked me up from work at 7:30pm and we drove down to Devon for a training session with Pete at a local pool. He was going to teach us vital capsize and recovery techniques that we hopefully wouldn't need in the summer but had better know just in case.

We spent 3 hours tipping out of our Kayaks and struggling to climb back into them. I couldn't even begin to imagine how much harder this was going to be should it happen in the middle of a fast-moving river where you can't put your feet on the bottom

Pete must have had a great afternoon's entertainment at our expense, as to begin with we were pretty rubbish and spend most of the time looking like a Koala bear hugging a kayak as it rolled us over. We were determined though and after several hours we eventually mastered the skill. By the end of the session, I felt confident of what to do in the event of a capsize, and I also discovered that I could quite easily paddle in a straight line. Pete explained to me how the kayaks we had borrowed for our first training session were for white water and therefore made to be easily moveable rather than staying in a straight line. Whereas the ones we were using with him were 'cross over' designed for longer distances and therefore to go straight. Result! I didn't suck at Kayaking.

We later discovered that the kayaks we had borrowed from the scout group and would be using for our training sessions had what is known as a 'skeg' on them. This is something you can drop down from underneath the boat into the water to help keep the boat going in a straight line. Safe to say once we discovered this there were no more training sessions where I spent my time zig zagging down the canal.

Throughout the months leading up to the trip we spent what little time we could in our kayaks, perfecting our techniques and increasing our stamina. In total we spent approximately 7 afternoons on the canal, paddling up and down, pulling the kayaks out of the water and walking around the locks. Hardly the top end training you would expect for a planned 60-day adventure down a 2350-mile-long river, but it was all we could manage, and any training was better than none.

The months were ticking down, and we were soon into June. I had one last piece of university work to finish to complete my Degree work and that was taking up lots of my time. Training was having to take a back seat and as July arrived so did the feeling of stress. I had a 4-day long diving competition to attend at the beginning of the month, auditions for a stage show that I was performing in, plus I had been selected as a volunteer at the Commonwealth Games in Glasgow towards the end of the month.

There was also the not so small matter of buying all the last-minute gear I would need for the trip. All this with less than 30 days to go before I flew out to America.

A few months previously Ken had been contacted by a man called Jim Lewis, a resident of Grand Rapids in Northern Minnesota and a fellow kayaker himself. He had completed the Mississippi in stages with friends and had contacted Ken to offer advice but first and foremost his help.

Ken explained to me how Jim had offered us beds at his house before we set out on the journey in August. He would pick us both up from the airport, take us shopping wherever we needed to go and then drive us to Lake Itasca (the source of the river) on the 7th of August. Well, that was an offer we couldn't refuse. It wasn't until we were actually out there that we realised it was an 8-hour round journey to collect someone from Minneapolis St Paul airport and then return to Grand Rapids. Jim would be doing this twice, once to pick up Ken on the 29th of July, and me on the 5th August (we were having to fly out at separate times due to my commitment to the Commonwealth Games up until the 2nd August).

It won't take much for you to realise that a departure date of the 5th of August didn't leave me long to get home from Scotland and pack ready for the Mississippi. As soon as I completed my final shift at the Commonwealth Pool, I headed straight to the train station to begin my journey home. It was a shame I couldn't hang around a bit longer, as I had been told I was to be awarded a free ticket to the closing ceremony due to being a 'stand out' volunteer. It was frustrating to miss the opportunity, but I couldn't justify losing a day's packing.

Once home, I had 2 full days to complete my packing. My family and friends were coming around on the Sunday night for a 'bon voyage party', which would no doubt prove to be emotional, and my boyfriend Phil, had come down and would be staying until the Monday afternoon (he was working in the evening) to help me pack and then say goodbye until October.

Most of the Monday was spent either packing or having emotional breakdowns. It had finally hit me what I was going to do and how long I would be away, and as safe as I knew we would be I was worried. I'm sure anyone heading out on any adventure always has that niggling feeling in their mind that they may not come back. So, there I stood looking over all my kit thinking how on earth it would fit in a kayak? I suddenly burst into tears. Before I knew it, Phil was there consoling me. I must have looked like an idiot crying over what appeared to be nothing. He rang his work to tell them he would not be going in (sorry Phil's work) and promptly took me outside for a walk. As the sun set on the last few hours of the day I was filling with dread, not only did I have to fly to America alone, I would also have to say goodbye to Phil tonight, and my parents and brother tomorrow. I had spent months away whilst at university, but this was different, I was safe there.

A few more tear-filled hours passed, and Phil said he needed to head home…well that was it I was off again. I couldn't cope, I couldn't say goodbye to him now, I couldn't draw out the process of all the goodbyes. I asked him to stay over and come to the airport, he refused saying it wasn't his place to be there. (In his defense we had only been together a few months at this point) The next thing I knew my Mum had talked to him out of my ear shot saying he had as much right to be there as anyone else and should come. He did. Thanks Mum.

5.45 am Tuesday 5th August. D Day.

Well, the day had arrived, I woke somewhat unenthusiastically, tried my best to eat what food I could, and helped by the fact that I slept most of the way there, before I knew it, we were at the airport.

Check in went smoothly and was actually entertaining when I was asked what business I had in the states…"I'm off to kayak the Mississippi river" probably wasn't the answer the man at the check in desk was expecting as his eyes opened wide.

After a quick drink at the café, where my mum accidently threw her coffee over everyone (sometimes I wonder where I get my gracefulness from), it was time to say goodbye. It was as hard as I thought it would be, but I got through it…just. I headed away up the stairs and didn't glance back. I was on my own now and I had to 'woman up'.

Once I hit 'security' I felt calm, almost as though the worst bit was over, I was starting to feel excited instead. I had timed my check in to perfection as by the time I had got though security my plane was boarding, and I walked straight on. As any long-haul flight does, it felt to take an age. I slept a bit and struck up a conversation with one of the flight attendants who had spotted the Rotary logo on my tee shirt and was interested in what I was doing, again cue the look of shock when I told him I was about to go and kayak the 4th longest river in the world.

I arrived at Washington airport, completed my transfer and before I knew it had arrived in Minneapolis and was texting Ken to say I was in baggage reclaim. Here I met Jim (the guy I mentioned earlier, who had offered to help us out) who shook my hand took my bag off me and told me to hop in the car alongside Ken. After a quick catch up, Ken broke the first bit of news to me …

"We called at Lake Itasca today before coming to get you and I'm afraid I have some bad news…the first 2 miles of the river are closed…"

What. I felt gutted, before we'd even started, we would be unable to complete all of the river, yes it was only 2 miles, but it was the very first bit. I started to feel like this was a sign that we shouldn't be going but I shook it off and we carried on in conversation. I must have slept for most of the journey as I only remember stopping for a bite at Subway and then being told we had arrived at Jim's house a full 24 hours after I had set off…bed time!

So, there I was in America. As I awoke the next morning and took everything in, I saw just how beautiful Jim's house was, not only inside but outside too and I went off to explore the latter. After a quick breakfast it was time to meet my Kayak. (Both mine and Ken's boats had been made in Washington State and shipped to Jim's on his request so he could look after them for us). There it was! Glowing bright red with not a scratch to be seen and it was mine. I quickly opened all the hatches and fully explored my new home-to-be for the next 60 days. Ken had named his boat OLLI (One Life Live It). I had been thinking over and over about a name for mine; someone back home had jokingly suggested YOLO (You Only Live Once). However annoying that phrase can be when some people use it, it seemed appropriate for this journey and so my boat was christened YOLO-LA, the

LA for no other reason than to make it sound better.

I unpacked all my gear in my room and began sorting everything out into bags and piles. I was impressed with myself as I tend to have a knack of packing unnecessary things for trips like this, such as when I had climbed Mt. Kilimanjaro I was advised to take a book, which I did, but I never used it, as was the case with a few other items. However, with this trip almost everything I brought was essential, I had only the smallest bag of extras that included a few home comforts. I didn't even have a book with me. I was more amazed to discover I could fit all my kit into my kayak comfortably and still had over half the back hatch available for food. I almost felt proud with how little I had brought.

Our next job was to go and buy our last-minute provisions and of course most importantly food. It was off to the Cub Foods and Target stores in Grand Rapids. Just some of the items we bought included 5 dehydrated meals each made up of rice or pasta, 3 lots of Idaho mashed potato, 2 sachets of tuna, a packet of 'trail mix' which was basically small packets of nuts, raisins and M&M's, 5 PowerAde's and two 10 litre bottles of water each. Alongside the food we also picked up a Jet Boil, sun cream, toilet roll, food tubs, plastic bottles, numerous tablets and first aid equipment amongst other things. This all needed to go in my boat somehow. On return to Jim's home I finished off my packing and the layout of my kayak was:-

Front Hatch: Laptop in several dry bags pushed up against the footrest; trainers pushed up to the front of one side of the bow Powerade bottles up the other; two boxes of wires and plugs for all my electrical gear; toilet roll; and a dry bag/rucksack.

Back Hatch: Tent pushed up against the back of the seat; sleeping mat rolled up and pushed into the back point of the boat; sleeping bag; thermals and pillows all in a dry bag next to the tent; a small bag of clothes which included a spare t-shirt and a pair of trousers that zipped into shorts; a smart set of shorts and my Mississippi top which I would wear when around other people; 2 pairs of socks and 5 lots of underwear (yes that's all). Food and my plastic tub which I would eat out of also went in this hatch.

Deck Bag: (on top of the kayak directly in front of me) Passport and other valuable items; digital camera and Go Pro accessories; maps; kagoule; snacks; my diary and Julien my lucky goat that Phil had given me.

Cockpit: Behind the seat were the 2 x10 litre bottles of water, along with two smaller ones, and to the side of me sun cream and bug spray.

My boat was almost packed, I had my last shower for an unknown number of days and changed into my paddling gear so I could wash and then pack my other clothes. Before I knew it, the time was nearing midnight, so it was time to head to bed. I had one last check and charge of all my electrical items, replied to a few emails, had a last chat with my parents and brother and then Phil, who told me he would send me an email a day for me to read as it would give him something to do, and me something nice to wake up to every morning. He sent email 1 of 60 that night. I clambered into bed before day 1 of my adventure began….

So here we are, and hopefully you are still with me as this is where the real adventure begins. The rest of this book is based on what I wrote in my diary after each day on the river, padded out so it's understandable, and hopefully more interesting than me just ranting with a pen over many pages. I have however, left in some snippets from my diary and these appear scattered throughout the story in italics. Anyway, back to the story… enjoy.

PART 2:
LAKE ITASCA TO GRAND RAPIDS

"He who is not courageous enough to take risks will accomplish nothing in life."
Muhammad Ali

CHAPTER 2
HEAVEN AND HELL IN A KAYAK

"Well it's safe to say today has been a mixed bag of emotions, excitement at the start of the day as it was time for our adventure to begin, but also tears as we battled through reeds, sandbars, beaver dams and many other things"

Thursday 7th August 2014. Coffee Pot Landing

It was time, the day had arrived, and our journey was about to begin! I awoke early to finish up my last-minute packing and before I knew it, we were in the car heading to Lake Itasca. It was a long journey in which we passed many sections of the river. A major part being Cass Lake and WOW! it looked huge, and that wasn't even the biggest lake we would be going across. All I could see was miles of water and a cluster of islands in the middle of it all. It was hard to believe that at some point that week we would be attempting to cross it.

On the approach to Itasca State Park Jim pulled the car over on a bridge going directly over a stream. I gave him a look as if to say, "what am I looking at?" He simply replied, "there you go that's the Mississippi River". I laughed, as I knew he wasn't joking. I had seen pictures and videos of the river at this point, but they had never done it justice. I knew it was going to be small, but I wasn't expecting a stream a metre wide and less than ankle deep. Everything just seemed so surreal. Were Ken and I actually going to do this....?

We parked the car and headed off to take some pictures of the official sign signalling the start of the river. As we headed towards this, we passed the information centre, a large 3D map of the Mississippi, and crowds of Americans enjoying their summer break. Pictures duly taken; I did the obligatory Social Media uploads to let everyone know that our adventure was on the way. This felt momentous as I was aware it could be my last contact with civilisation for a while.

We enquired with some park staff as to where we could actually put our kayaks in the river due to the first 2 miles being closed off. We had spotted a bridge with a steep bank down to the water and asked if this would be okay, it was. We were happy to find out putting in here meant we would only miss out 800ft of the river in total. Maybe everything wasn't stacked against us after all.

Next, the not so easy task of carrying our kayaks to the river. You probably imagine us pulling up the car next to the river, sliding the Kayaks into the water and paddling into the sunset…it was nothing like that.

We unloaded the Kayaks from the trailer and proceeded to work out how to use the portage wheels. We had bought these after being advised that they would make any portages we had to do easier. (A portage is when you have to pull your boat out of the water, walk it around the obstacle e.g. a lock and then put it back in at the other side.)

We had a second occurrence of the "that's not going anywhere" speech as within 200 metres of the car the wheels slid from underneath one of the boats and we had to start over.

Wheels re-attached we began to pull the boats towards the bridge a few thousand feet away. With each kayak weighing about 90 kilograms this was no mean feat. It was no surprise I overheard a member of the public asking a member of park about what we were doing with…?

 "they will be attempting to get to the Gulf, lot's try but hardly any make it". Was his reply.

After an hour of pulling pushing and lifting we finally had our kayaks at the top of the riverbank. A large crowd of people had gathered on the bridge above us, each asking where we were going and offering words of encouragement.

We somehow managed to lift each boat down into the water, and as I stepped into the river for the first time the water only just rippled over the top of my crocs. We weren't going to be paddling any time soon. We must have looked ridiculous stood there pulling on buoyancy aids whilst being stood only ankle deep in water.

All kit on. Julian my lucky goat fixed in place. A crowd of excited Americans cheering. The moment had arrived, and we were ready to go. We pulled the boats under the bridge to where the water looked slightly deeper and said our goodbyes to Jim. I took my seat in what was to be my home for the next 60 days. My first paddle stroke was greeted with an even louder cheer from the crowd…and we were off…it felt great, finally after all this planning we were underway.

No sooner had I let out a smile than I came to an abrupt stop, I had struck bottom, the crowd behind us started to laugh as I scrambled out of my kayak and began to push it along.

As we rounded the first corner of the river we could hear someone in the crowd shout out

"You'll never make it!"

I turned to Ken, we both laughed and shouted back

"We will see you at the Gulf".

I will never know which person shouted out from deep within the group of people but one thing I knew then was that however random of a pairing we looked, Ken and I were not to be underestimated. We had said we would do this, so we would.

At first 'walking' and pushing our kayaks seemed quite funny; we managed about 10 paddle strokes before having to heave ourselves out and pull them behind us on a rope. After a few hours the novelty very quickly wore off, particularly as the back of my legs became bruised and tender from constantly getting in and out of my kayak. Each time my kayak stopped I let out a groan as I prepared for the pain to begin again.

Neither Ken nor I could have foreseen what lay immediately ahead.

A few hours into our day we rounded a corner to meet a five-foot wall of reeds and thick bull rushes that stretched out as far as we could see, and my heart sank; I knew we had to go through it. Ken led the way as we pushed and pulled our way through the maze. The reeds cut my bare skin and it got harder and harder to paddle due to the thickness of them. Most of our time was spent physically grabbing hold of a clump of reeds and pulling ourselves through. Ken shouted out saying he was stuck and he was going to climb out to push his kayak. However, this was quickly followed by a panicked

"Don't get out, it's a bog underneath".

Suddenly I was hit by the stark realisation that we were alone and stuck in the middle of this maze of reeds and however hard I tried I couldn't move myself forward. I was stranded! I did my best not to panic, but as someone who is slightly claustrophobic this was hard, and I would be lying if I said it didn't cross my mind that it would be extremely difficult, if not impossible, for anyone to find or see us amongst the reeds. If needed, how could we be rescued?

Much to my relief some two hours later we finally broke through the reeds and we were free. That type of environment was certainly not what I had expected.

The river started to open up slightly and it was back to the routine of paddling a bit and walking the rest. Our progress was hampered by sandbars, rocks or beaver dams. With each bump and scrape slowly reducing my motivation and enthusiasm for the journey ahead.

We had been pulling our kayaks for miles when I tripped over a rock and landed flat in the water, cutting my legs up in the process. I was cold, wet, and tired. I wanted and needed to reach camp. It was 6.30pm, we had 2 hours of daylight left with 6 miles still to go. I was worried. Our current pace meant we would be paddling in the dark, in treacherous conditions, and would reach camp exhausted to be then faced with putting up our tents with only the moonlight to help us.

We continued as the river tightly meandered back and forth, scrambling in and out of our kayaks every few minutes. We were both still struggling to get to grips with our paddling strokes and our steering. It was difficult to turn a 15ft kayak in the narrow bends of the river. Our paddling technique resembled that of punting; digging in sharply with our shoulders to negotiate the sharp turns.

The clock ticked on to 7.00 pm and we continued to punt along at a slow pace. At one point I completely misjudged a turn and went straight onto a sandbar. I attempted to shuffle myself free, but it was hopeless. I decided the only way to get free was to climb out and hope that without my weight the kayak would break free. I stepped out of the kayak with one foot…and suddenly my whole leg sank. I was hip deep into the sand, completely stuck – one leg consumed by the sand and the other still in the kayak – wondering what could I do now? I shouted to Ken in panic. As I tried to pull my leg free from the sand. I was sinking deeper and I could feel my shoe slipping off my foot. Ken came to my rescue sticking his paddle down into the sand. Although this hit my foot, he did succeed in dislodging the sand allowing me to pull myself and my shoe free. I was incredibly shaken by the whole experience and this, along with tiredness from having had only one day to get used to the time difference, and stress from our current situation, caused my emotions to get the better of me; I began to well up and streams of tears began to fall. I really wanted to go home.

We continued, negotiating our way around what felt like 100 corners hoping at each one we would see our campsite. Each time we just saw another stretch of river, and my heart would sink. However, eventually the moment came, and I turned to see the signpost that signalled our stopping point for the night. I let out a huge sigh of relief as I pulled up on to the bank. I could make out two dark figures at the top side of the campsite. They cheered as we arrived, and one came running down, grabbed my kayak, and pulled me ashore. He introduced himself as Critter before going to help Ken. He generously offered us the warmth of his fire and helped us with our kit. We were introduced to Yvonne (also called Critter) – the second dark figure and his paddling partner - before setting up camp.

Ken began cooking our evening meal and I put up each of our two tents. Our meal was set out under the light of the moon and fire. Although I had been so hungry, I was unable to eat the rice Ken had made. I felt sick and couldn't stomach it. Mindful of the need to keep wild animals at bay I disposed of the food by throwing it into a bush at the top end of the site as this would help ensure our personal safety during the night. I now hung my wet clothes out to dry in the small hut provided at the camp. The only other 'luxury' was the toilet, housed in a shack on site.

The fire provided some relief from the cold night. Critter and Yvonne intimated that they were toasting some marshmallows on the fire and invited us to join them. This was a hoax. There were no marshmallows on sticks, but there were fire eating sticks! We were treated to our own private fire breathing/eating display. To say this was a surprise is an understatement! I had certainly not expected this on my first, or any night of this challenge.

The fire display had given me some temporary respite from the emotional turmoil of the day. However, this was brief and as I turned in for the night I collapsed onto the floor of my tent, exhausted and desperate for sleep. Emotion overcame me and as I heard the fire crackling behind me the tears began to roll down my face. What had I let myself in for?

To say I was less than enthusiastic to carry on the journey is no exaggeration. I woke several times during the night in a blind panic. I struggled to breath. I felt so alone. I was extremely disorientated – not knowing where I was.

After a rough night sleep Ken and I emerged from our tents at 8:30am the following morning to see the sun shining and a morning mist on the river. This failed to brighten my mood. All I could think about was how this was only our second day ...there were 58 more to go.

I couldn't stomach any breakfast. I felt sick, tired, and mentally drained. I just wanted to go home and if someone had arrived at the campsite saying they had a car to take us away, I would have gone. However, this wasn't going to happen so there was nothing for it but to get my head down and crack on.

Having broken camp, the first task for the day was to carry our kayaks to the river. This was a journey in itself. We had to carry them to the top of the campsite, down a road, over a bridge and down a slope into the water. This was made necessary due to the local wildlife (beavers) having built a dam across the exit of the campsite. At this point we weren't exactly appreciative of their efforts. The second task was to re pack our things into the kayaks. We were both still learning how best to pack the boats, so it was a slow process. Some two hours later after plenty of lifting, pushing and pulling, we were back in our kayaks and ready to continue our journey.

Once back on the river, my spirits lifted, and I felt ready to face the day. I told myself to 'man up' and off we paddled. An eagle suddenly flew out of a nearby tree circled around us a couple of times and flew off in the direction of the river almost as if guiding our way. We passed through some wonderful scenery and were fortunate to see other wildlife such as beavers, and numerous birds. Unfamiliar and strange howling halfway through the day was less welcome but did increase my paddling speed and spur me on in my journey!

As the day progressed, I began to feel my arms and legs burning from the sun. I applied more of my factor 75(+) sun cream. I did this process multiple times a day due to the cream getting washed off by the water.

There was an endless line of obstacles in our path that day. Ken and I had once again to force our way through miles and miles of dense vegetation. I was extremely wet from clambering in and out of my kayak to manoeuvre my way through. Bugs were having a field day biting us at every opportunity, making my skin itchy and irritating.

Later, in the day we found our path blocked off by a fallen tree. I let out a groan as it looked impassable; it was half submerged in the water and spanned the whole width of the river I wondered how on earth we could negotiate it. On closer inspection we could make out where previous boats had forced a way over the trunk. Leading the way, I built up as much speed as I could to force my way through. As I reached the trunk I came to an abrupt halt. I couldn't get through. I was stuck and going nowhere. I laughed and quickly tried to think of a way over the tree. The water was suddenly deep, and I was not about to dive in and take my chances. I scrambled out of my Kayak and balancing on the tree trunk pulled my kayak through my legs. My next trick was to manoeuvre myself back into my kayak. I had to time this to perfection. I finished pulling my kayak through and waited until it was moving freely with the flow of the water. I then dived on to the top feet first, sliding my legs into the cockpit as I went. The manoeuvre would surely have impressed any bystander had there been anyone around to see.

We aimed to stop at a Department of Natural Resources (DNR) campsite named Pine Point, clearly labelled on our map at 17 miles. After we had paddled about 15 miles (according to our GPS) I spotted what looked like a well-used banking on the right, where the grass was flattened as though boats had pulled up on it numerous times. Behind it a small path wound its way up onto a hill. I shouted out to Ken who had just paddled past telling him I thought this may be our stop. He wasn't sure, to be fair neither was I, as according to the map we still had at least 2 miles to go.

We stopped for a moment to assess our situation, should we pull up here onto what may be private property or, go down stream 2 more miles and find the campsite. The decision was made to carry on paddling a further 2 miles and if we couldn't find our planned stop, we would come back up stream to this point.

We paddled further and further praying we would find the site on every turn, but we passed no dry ground. As the sun was now beginning to set, we had to make the decision to turn back. Paddling upstream was challenging work and frustrating knowing we would be paddling back down the same section the next morning.

Thankfully we spotted the ground I had pointed out earlier, pulled ashore and christened it Pine Point. In all fairness it was on a hill at a bend in the river and therefore a 'point' …and there were pine trees on it, so that was good enough for us. (It should be pointed out that we later discovered it had been a sensible decision to turn back as the real Pine Point campsite is no longer accessible from the river due to vegetation, meaning we never would have found it. The land we camped on was indeed private property.)

We emptied our boats and carried our gear up the hill. Once camp was set-up I was suddenly overwhelmed by a feeling of loneliness as once again we were cut off from the world, and no one was close by or probably even knew we were there. Raised high above the river we both approached the edge to look out on our view for the first time and the sight that met our eyes made us both feel sick. For miles on end all we could see was vegetation several feet high covering the full expanse of the valley. The river itself could not be seen apart from the small stretch leading into the rushes below, but we knew it was there somewhere, and tomorrow we would have to go through it.

Feeling incredibly un-motivated, I pitched my tent and crawled inside to rest my aching limbs and nurse my numerous insect bites. I pulled out my phone and amazingly I had a signal, my first thought was to ring my family, but I doubted I would hold myself together, so I rang Phil instead. I was 'balling my eyes out' to him, saying how desperately alone I felt, how everything hurt, and how there was no way I could carry on. My emotions were so raw, and I couldn't control myself. Phil tried to console me, but I would say it was pretty impossible. I hung up my phone and slowly walked back to camp. There was no hiding my tears from Ken as he waited for me to return, I offered him my phone so he could talk to Pauline (his wife) as he had no signal, he declined, and we ate our food in silence.

After food Ken and I began to discuss how we were feeling. We both agreed how ironic it was that people imagined us to be having the time of our lives, building campfires, waving to bears on the riverbank, laughing and joking away. The reality couldn't have been more different, we felt like the only people on the planet.

Moments later we heard shouting in the distance. We both stood up to see Critter and Yvonne paddling towards us, we shouted down to tell them this was the only dry ground for at least 2 miles (they too were trying to find Pine Point) and how they should probably stop here for the night. They pulled ashore and we returned their favour from the previous night by helping them take their gear up to the camp. After a quick reunion, catch up of the day's events, and removing a tick from my arm, I could hear my bed calling. I was soon fast asleep, dreading the next day's events.

As I ventured out of my tent at 6.30 am the next morning the never-ending green maze below was covered in mist. We had a long day ahead. Ken had set our aim for the day as Stump Lake and a campsite nearby, some 25 miles away. I was sure this was far too ambitious for us so early on in the journey and said as much.

We were on the water two hours after waking up (already faster than the first day) and it was time to take on 'the maze' that we had now aptly named 'the green hell'. My moods fluctuated throughout the day and it was hard to stay motivated.

We paddled for hours in what felt like a never-ending world of green. I could just make out trees over the top of the rushes in either direction. It felt almost like we were boxed in, as though we were the small ball in the children's puzzle game where you tip the maze to roll the ball into the centre. Whichever way we turned the rushes continued.

Eventually late in the afternoon they ceased, only to be replaced by fallen trees from both sides of the river, which we had to go under, over and through. Up until this point we had been making great time but now our aim of Stump Lake was nigh on impossible. Whilst stuck under a tree I heard a voice shouting from the bank. A local of the area was informing Ken that the DNR had recently been down the river cutting a way through the trees… (how thoughtful of them, or not) …indeed they had cut holes in the trees, but as they had cut off each tree's roots this meant now our path was that of a zigzag, one tree on the left of the river, the other on the right. Oh well every cloud and all that….

I finally managed to loosen whatever it was keeping me trapped under that particular tree and proceeded to the next one. I soon managed to come up with a system and technique for negotiating them swiftly. If I lined up my kayak as much as possible with the 'hole' and paddled full pelt at it, I would (fingers crossed) have enough speed to get over the tree trunk or quickly duck down into my Kayak and pass under the low-lying branches in one go. A great technique, that is if I could turn my kayak into the correct position in the small space available and avoid getting hit by rogue branches. This continued for around 3 hours until I heard a strange noise.

'What's that' I exclaimed to Ken.

'No idea' was his reply

We carried on paddling in the direction of the noise and as a few more meanders of the river brought us closer I realised it was music. It was getting louder and louder, and as the rushes cleared Ken let out a laugh in front of me.

"What's up" I asked?

"You need to see this" was his reply.

As I caught up with him, I couldn't believe my eyes… We knew from our map that we should soon be approaching a place called Lake Irvin and I was excited to get out of the 'green hell' as I felt like it had been days since we had been near civilisation, or even on the same planet as other people.

However, I had never expected it to be quite like it was.

Once I turned the corner, the rushes and trees disappeared and there in front of me were over 100 people partying in the middle of the lake. Okay, so on closer inspection they weren't actually in the middle of the lake, they were on a huge sandbar playing volleyball and drinking beers. One particular family were sat around a table on chairs shin deep in water, of course once they caught the sound of our voices and realised that we were British they struck up a friendly conversation and wanted to know what we were doing. We took a few minutes break as we chatted away to them, I wanted to accept their kind invitation to join them but instead we had to begin our-mile-long crossing to the other side of Lake Irving.

At about a mile by a mile and a half wide, Lake Irvin was the smallest of the lakes we would cross on this journey. I had never been on such a big expanse of water in a Kayak and it felt quite daunting, but we went full speed ahead and we crossed it in fifteen minutes. From Lake Irvin we went straight onto Lake Bemidji where we decided we had better look for a hotel for the night as the sun was beginning to set and there was no campsite close by. We pulled up on a beach and I promptly collapsed onto the sand in exhaustion.

I stayed with the boats as Ken set off in the direction of a few hotels hoping that one would have room for us. He must have looked quite the sight in his buoyancy aid and splash skirt.

Ken soon returned and confirmed that one of the hotels had space for us. So relieved, we gutted our Kayaks and took all but the boats themselves into the hotel as we didn't want to risk having any kit stolen. After a shower and a change of clothes we headed out to explore what Bemidji had to offer, which wasn't much. Apparently, we had chosen the wrong end of town and most of the restaurants and bars were on the other side of the lake. However, we bought an ice cream from a hut and sat down overlooking the lake. Ken let out a chuckle…

"Is it just me or is this ridiculous? Two hours ago, I was stuck under a tree, now I'm sat in the sunshine, overlooking a huge, beautiful lake, eating ice cream!"

The craziness of the situation was not lost on me and I laughed along. We began to talk about our plans for the morning, Ken was keen on us making up for the miles we hadn't manage to cover that day. He began making calls to see if someone would be able to give us a lift to the other side of the lake to help us make up for lost time. After a while and not much luck, I suggested giving it up as a lost cause; we were only behind 5 miles and I was sure we could make it up if we got on the lake a bit earlier in the morning. I didn't think we needed to panic just yet as 5 miles was the equivalent of about an hour and a quarter of paddling and I was sure we could cope.

Back in the hotel, after a good meal, I was looking forward to sleeping in a proper bed again. My shoulder had started to ache over the last few days so I was hoping a night off the floor may do it some good. I had a quick catch up with family and then it was time for bed.

CHAPTER 3
CROSSING THE OPEN WORLD

"If I could freeze a moment in time it would be this moment. I am currently sat on the edge of Star Island in the middle of Cass Lake and apart from the waves crashing up against the shore it is peaceful. Looking out I can see only some of the distance we have to come, this lake is huge and to think we must have spent 2 hours on it already and we are only half way. I can just about make out where we are heading, but that is tomorrows challenge." **Sunday 10th August 2014. Star Island.**

Over the next few days' time was spent either meandering through the green hell or crossing many lakes. My shoulder was getting worse by the day and was sending stabbing pains up into my neck and down my back.

You could be forgiven for thinking lakes would be simple to navigate. Surely if you know where you are going you just point towards it and paddle…but that could not be more wrong. When a lake is so big you cannot see the other side, it becomes very lonely and disorientating. Along with this the Mississippi seemed to have a knack of making things as difficult as possible for us, an example being in the middle of Lake Bemidji we came across a huge area of bull rushes and wild rice blocking our path. Paddling around wasn't an option as it was so big, instead we had to go through it and by the time we broke free at the other side we were completely disoriented so much so that we had to ask a group of local fishermen to find out where the river actually began again, which seemed to amuse them as they pointed out a small opening to the north of us.

These types of situation recurred on many of the lakes. We would always be amazed by the vastness of each one and then began squinting our eyes to locate where the discharge into the river was.

We crossed Stump and Wolf Lakes with little event, and all was going well until around halfway across Andrusia Lake, when the heavens opened. We had seen the storm ahead, but Ken was adamant it was going in the opposite direction, on reflection that was probably very much a hope and a way to try and keep us both calm.

My first experience of kayaking in the rain was nothing short of terrifying, as thunder rumbled around us and lightning lit up the sky, we picked up our pace and bee-lined for the bridge that signalled the end of our crossing. Paddling as fast as I could I felt rubbing on my hands where I was gripping my paddle and small blisters were beginning to form, I tried to ignore the pain and just focused on my goal. Thankfully, we made it across the lake unscathed, it seemed our change in speed had been worth it as we sheltered from the onslaught of rain that soon followed. Being on a wide-open expanse of water with lightening over our heads was not something we wanted to repeat.

As the rain cleared slightly, we moved off in the direction of our next Lake. Unfortunately, the rain didn't stop for long, and it followed us all the way to the edge of Cass Lake. This was the Lake Jim had pointed out to us on our drive to the headwaters and if it had looked big then, it was gigantic now. I set about scanning the horizon to pick out the island we were planning on camping on…

"Is that the island we are aiming for" I shouted across to Ken whilst pointing at the huge island about a mile across.

"No that's Potato Island (yes, really, Potato Island). There's another island behind that and then ours is the one after that."

"Oh!" I replied.

Cass Lake really was huge, and it took us over two hours to reach Star Island and our campsite for the night. Cold and wet we eventually pulled up onto the beach to find we had stepped foot onto the set of a horror film!

"Erm…., Ken have you seen this?"

"What?"

I had ventured ahead to scout the site. There were two big sandy areas for pitching tents and a 'loo' further down a path to the other side of the island. As I went through to the next patch of sand, up ahead I could see tents pitched. I was instantly uplifted with the thought of being able to talk to other people which made being cold and wet a little less depressing.

However, on closer inspection I discovered all the tents were deserted. I called out, but no one answered. Clothes, toilet roll, and cooking equipment were scattered around the ground as though people had left in a hurry. It seemed people had been here recently but where were they now? The tents were flapping in the wind as their doors had been left open. My feelings of happiness suddenly disappeared as I surveyed the scene. What had happened here?

"So Ken, this is a bit creepy!"

"Agreed, let's pitch up back there by the beach and see if anyone turns up"

I backed away from the tents with the reed knife from my buoyancy aid close at hand and walked back towards Ken. We chose to set our tents up as far away from the others as possible just in case. Thankfully the rain soon stopped and with the sun beginning to shine I took the time to use the safety line attached to my Kayak as a makeshift washing line. I fixed it to two trees and hung out my wet clothes.

Home for the night set up, we both crawled into our '1st class accommodation' AKA our tents. It hadn't been a bad day in all, the lakes were a break from the monotony of the winding river and the view from our camp was spectacular which lifted my spirits.

About half an hour later I decided to visit the water's edge and as I popped my head out of my tent, I saw a man stood near one of the other tents across the way. Of course, he was there to attack me and that was the only thought that raced through my head as soon as I saw him.

Safe to say this didn't happen, instead he introduced himself and explained to us how the tents were his. Apparently, the site at the other side of the island was full so he and his friends were merely sleeping here but spending time with family from the other camp during the day, hence the reason for very empty tents. I still wasn't sure why this meant their belongings were all over the floor but maybe they had just been blown around by the weather, anyway the panic was over.

We were treated to a beautiful sunset that evening as we sat on the beach writing our journals and cooking our tea. It was relaxing listening to the waves lap against the shore and for the first time in days I felt relaxed and happy.

I knew the next day was going to be tough as we had to cross Lake Winnibigoshish (Lake Winni) a 13-mile-wide man made 'lake' (at that width I don't see how it can be a lake and not an inland sea) and as I watched the sun go below the horizon, I felt a sense of dread begin to build in my stomach. I soon pushed it away as I told myself to just take it all one step at a time, we still had to get off Cass Lake and then cover several miles before we even got near Lake Winni. Worrying about it right then wasn't going to help anything. I headed to bed with my newfound calmness.

Whoosh…crash…whoosh…crash!

I knew as I laid awake the next morning that that sound could mean only one thing, wind and waves. I was right. I clambered out of my tent to be met with the sight of white capped waves crashing into the shore, they weren't huge by any stretch of the imagination, maybe 3 foot tall, and had I been on holiday at the beach I would have probably dived right into them. However, negotiating these in a Kayak would be a bit different as once sat down the waves would be almost the same height as us.

Knowing we had a fight ahead of us we collapsed our tents and packed up the boats in record time. There was a good chance that the morning's paddle would now take longer than planned so we didn't want to waste any time. Thankfully my clothes had dried out quite well and it was now time to get ourselves back in the boats.

In a normal situation this would be very easy, and I would just put my legs either side of my kayak, stabilise the cockpit with my hands, drop my bum in and then awkwardly pull my legs inside. This I feared, in these waves would be difficult, but I was going to give it my best shot.

I waded out into the waves until my Kayak was off the sand and was instantly soaked to the skin. I had my boat side on in front of me as I tried to push it against the waves, and it wasn't long until I was swept off my feet and onto my back in the water.

Once back on my feet, I assumed my position, legs either side of the kayak stabilising the cockpit with my hands as the waves started to push the kayak into my right leg almost knocking me over again. I managed to regain my balance and hop into my boat as a three-foot swell flooded my kayak, out I climbed and tipped out the water. I looked over to Ken who was finding it just as difficult and we both began to laugh. In the end we decided to go for the long tried and tested technique of clambering into our boats on shore, fixing our splash skirts into place and shuffling into the water. It took a long time but was successful none-the-less.

Finally off the shore, we began paddling around the headland of the island we had just left in search of the opening back onto the river. High swells and a headwind made this hard work, and we were making little progress. We were desperately scanning the horizon for some sign of an opening and many times we thought we had found it only to realise it was actually just a cove. I pulled out binoculars from my deck bag, but every time I raised them to my eyes a wave would roll over my boat and attempt to tip me out, or I would bob up and down so much that seeing anything through them was nigh on impossible.

Ken managed to get out the maps and we marked an approximate current location. If this was correct the opening would be to the east of where we were currently. I turned my head and scanned the shore and there it was, Knutson Dam as straight east as could be. We turned our boats and continued to battle against the waves in the general direction of the dam and campsite.

After what felt like a lifetime, we finally made it. Once my Kayak was ashore, I collapsed on the ground exhausted. Given how much energy the crossing had taken out of us we decided to have a well-earned 30-minute break.

Here we met Marlin who was a local and brother of the owner of the campsite next to the dam. He approached me and asked what I was doing. It was the first time someone had not so much as flinched when I replied. It was almost refreshing. He then proceeded to tell me how he had dropped his three-foot-long machete and was now looking for it…yes, as casual as that! I still wonder to this day how you can just drop and loose a three-foot-long machete.

We had a good chat with Marlin as he moved around eyes peeled to the ground signalling with his hands the size of his lost item. We found out all about his life and he showed us the scars from where he had been shot and stabbed multiple times, this kind of helped to explain the machete situation. I still do wonder whether he ever found it.

After our break it was time to get back onto the river and face the big momma of the lakes, Lake Winni. It was going to take us a good few hours to reach it but we knew it was coming and our anxiety began to build as it was the 4th biggest lake in Minnesota and we were going to have to cross it one way or another.

From day one Lake Winni had been 'bigged up' as a big moment in the journey and as such was probably the reason from mine and Ken's nervousness. A lot of people had been quick to advise us against going across the middle due to the easily changeable weather systems that it could create halfway across, instead it was advised that we 'hug' the shore. This would add another 10 miles to our journey but would likely be the safest option. In contrast we had also spoken to a few people who had been a bit more gung-ho and paddled straight across safely. We had settled on making a decision on the day dependent on the conditions we were faced with.

We knew Winni was going to be big but that didn't stop my mouth dropping to the bottom of my Kayak as we paddled slowly into the opening. I could only see water in front of me. To the right, a tree lined shore extended away for miles on end and to the left, rocks formed a shore winding away from us. A young boy was bathing in the shallows only a few metres away. We sat for around 5 minutes in awe of the view ahead of us. This was man made!

It was now late in the afternoon and after our battle at Lake Cass we were behind schedule. We didn't feel it would be safe to go straight across in such a state of exhaustion, but we also didn't have time to paddle another 10 miles from our current location in the south west all the way around the headland to the north east. Instead, we made the decision to locate the campsite which was shown on the map as being just down the left banking near where the young boy was bathing. We would have the evening off and get up earlier than usual to negotiate Winni before noon.

Approaching the young boy, we discovered his family, who were sat on a ridge keeping an eye on him. They helped us ashore and advised us about the location of the campsite. They were staying there, and it was only a short walk away, so they insisted on showing us around.

On the 'tour' we spotted the Park Rangers who made a point of explaining about the system of paying for a camping spot; we simply needed to choose somewhere and then put some money in a post-box just up the road. They said that if we carried on further down the shore, there was a boat ramp we could use and that we could camp there. Well at least that's what Ken and I heard! She actually said 'can't', but we were poor Yorkshire folk and American accents were lost on us. An hour later our tents were pitched on a patch of grass just down from the boat ramp and right on the edge of Lake Winnibigoshish.

Before Ken and I set off on this adventure we had agreed on some rules that we would abide by all the way down the river:

1. Do not fall in – pretty self-explanatory really
2. No arguing in camp – regardless of how we felt or how much we wanted to scream at each other on the river all arguments would be left out there, the trip was going to be hard enough as it was without us refusing to talk to each other on our 'down time'.
3. Make all decisions together – again doesn't take much to figure this one out

Rule number 3 was put into action bright and early the next morning. At 5.30 am we looked out on a lake that looked more like a sheet of glass, we exchanged glances that said only one thing…lets go straight across!

I sat in my boat and pushed off from the shore. The only thing to be heard was mine and Ken's paddle strokes, and with the sun just showing its head and warming up the air I dug out my iPod put it on shuffle and began my paddle across the biggest lake on the Mississippi to MMMBop by Hansen. (Well done iPod)

6 miles in we could have been forgiven for regretting our decision to paddle straight across, the wind had picked up and the swells were tossing us around. Ken suggested breaking to the right and heading up the shore. A quick assessment told me this would mean us paddling into the wind and therefore probably for longer, so I suggested we kept our line to the headland about a mile way and then hugged the shore from there if needs be.

My suggestion paid off and after celebrating us completing our first 100 miles (a simple cheer after all we still had 2450 to go) we stopped on the top side of the headland around an hour later. To our relief we were now protected from the wind, so we decided to have a quick break before heading around and back down to the river. Here I had a remarkable experience.

I had been advised to buy a 'she wee' for this trip and I put it to the test for the first time at that moment, being able to stand up for the toilet was so much easier and meant less chance of getting bitten by bugs or scratched by all types of vegetation.

Triumphant wee completed we were back on the water and after what felt like an eternity we were at the dam. We pulled up onto shore to find a steep climb was in store for us to get over the dam and back onto the water.

Ken spotted what appeared to be a Dad with his two teenage sons and asked if they would help us. He pointed me out in the hope of enticing the young males into helping. I don't know how he thought this would help as I was dripping with sweat and river water; bug bites covered every bit of exposed skin and I needed a shower. Miraculously it worked and before I knew it the two young males had picked up my boat as though it was candyfloss and were carrying it up the slope and over the road to the other side of the dam.

It was then time for lunch as we congratulated each other on what we had just achieved. I felt a major sense of pride, Lake Winnibigoshish had been built up to be such a major and dangerous part of the journey and we had successfully conquered it!

10 miles left for the day and we were high on motivation and covering the miles quickly. Things were going well, too well, and it wasn't too long until this changed as I suddenly felt a stabbing pain on my left-hand side, I rubbed my hand against it and the pain went away only to come back minutes later, it was so sudden it made me jump and stop paddling.

Again, I felt my side this time my hands discovered a large lump. I quickly lifted up my splash skirt and t-shirt in panic thinking a tick was burying itself into me but instead I discovered a red spot. Ken came to inspect giving me the news that all the lower left side of my back and side was covered in red puss filled spots! I had been bitten, or should I say something had feasted on me. There wasn't much that could be done there and then apart from paddle on and get to a camping spot as soon as possible to treat them.

We arrived at a camp site (otherwise known as a patch of grass) with a boat ramp named Leech Lake landing. Pulling ashore we discovered the floor was moving.

Hundreds of green frogs were hidden in amongst the grass and we had disturbed them with our presence, they were now jumping around wildly trying to get away from us and it created the illusion that the floor was moving. We moved away from the frogs and towards an open space where after checking for frogs I dumped my kit on the ground and immediately reached for the first aid kit. Puss was flowing out of each spot and they were tender to touch, I tried to clean each one as best I could and applied tee tree oil to the area before covering it back up.

After erecting my tent, I turned to see a car pull up, my heart started to beat a bit faster thinking we were about to be thrown off the land. Thankfully we weren't. Instead, a lady who introduced herself as Sandy emerged from the car, she had been following us on Facebook since day one and has seen that were had stopped for the day at this site. She lived not far away so had come along to say hello and invite us to her house for pancakes in the morning. We didn't need asking twice and accepted her wonderful offer. Further conversation with Sandy told us we were only around 30 river miles away from Grand Rapids which was our stopping point for the week and where Jim lived (who we would once again be staying with for the night). Our spirits skyrocketed. 30 miles was only one more day of kayaking, we would be back where we had started in a matter of one day, and to top it off we would be having a good breakfast to start the day. Brilliant.

CHAPTER 4
THE BATTLE OF BLACKWATER

We were motivated and ready to go the next morning knowing we were only 30 miles from Grand Rapids and that a breakfast of pancakes was going to be provided by Sandy. Our spirits were high, and we were moving quickly. It soon turned out that Sandys house wasn't quite as close as we had hoped, on and on we paddled, expecting to see her house around every corner.

Hunger and maybe a bit of hysteria was setting as we both began shouting out Sandy's name at the top of our lungs desperate to stop and get some food in us. I felt to have no energy and every paddle stroke was taking maximum effort.

Finally, after what felt like an eternity of meanders, we made it to Sandy's house, that by now we had nicknamed the 'pancake house'. Sandy met us at the river's edge with a sign welcoming us by name and invited us warmly into her house. We discussed the past few days' adventure, and in particular our crossing of Lake Winnibigoshish and my bites, to which we were all at a loss as to what they were from. We then stuffed our faces with pancakes, and they were amazing.

The short break, friendly conversation, and pancake power was just what we needed to encourage us back onto the river. Before leaving Sandy suggested that she and her family come and pick us up that evening to take us to the County Fair that was taking place nearby, this sounded like a great idea and we happily accepted.

Once back on the water everything was going smoothly until the wild rice returned as we meandered across another lake named 'Blackwater Lake'. What should have been a simple 1-mile crossing turned into 3 miles of paddling backwards and forwards across the lake in wide sweeps.

Minnesota power station could be seen in the distance, but it never seemed to be getting any closer as we approached it from every possible angle. All we could do was carry on and wait for the 'green hell' to come to an end. After hours of paddling to and fro we made it to the far side of the lake and back onto the river where we started to keep an eye out for Pokegama

Dam, our stop for the day. We got ever closer to the buildings ahead of us and I could just make out the boat ramp. As the front of my kayak beached up onto the land. I sat in silence…1 week down, 7 to go.

That night Sandy and her family met us and took us to the County Fair. It was great to be up and about walking and surrounded by people. The chance to eat real food was not to be missed and I think it's fair to say that the hot dogs we ate had never tasted better. After looking at the animals and talking to a few locals it was time to head back to our tents. It felt incredibly strange to be in a car and bizarre to be travelling at 30 mph, after moving at a maximum of around 3mph for the last week. On arriving back at the dam both Ken and I let out a groan…our kayaks were still there and had not been stolen…we would have to keep going!

PART 3:
POKEGAMA DAM, GRAND RAPIDS –
MINNEAPOLIS

'Whatever the mind of man can conceive and believe, it can achieve' Napoleon Hill

CHAPTER 5
WEATHERING THE STORMS

Waking up the next morning knowing I did not have to get in a kayak and paddle was the most amazing feeling. Collapsing camp and having a Nutri-grain bar for breakfast did not seem half as monotonous or dull as all the other mornings, and we both sat happily discussing the week's events whilst surveying the river we had paddled down the previous day.

Our original idea had been to break camp early and paddle the 4 miles into central Grand Rapids and the next dam on the river. We were going to pull out there and secure our boats overnight, however a sign next to our camping spot that we had spotted the previous night soon put a stop to that.

The sign cautioned us on paddling the 4 miles stretch between this dam and the next due to treacherous waters and instead, advised phoning the power company who provide a portage service into town. (it was the power company who owned and operated the dam, as such they were required to operate this portaging service as they had blocked off the river) This seemed like a great arrangement to us, so Ken called the number and arranged our transport.

Within half an hour our kayaks were strapped to the trailer of a truck and we were on our way. The driver advised us against our initial plan of unloading the kayaks in town, and leaving them in a secure place, due to the high probability of them being stolen while we waited for Jim to come and collect us. Instead, he offered to drive us to Jim's house, so we happily accepted his offer.

On arrival at Jim's, we discovered he wasn't yet home. So, we hid all our gear out of sight and headed off in search of some shops to resupply. We figured that the sooner we got that done the more time we could spend relaxing. So, we walked to the shops just over a mile away, filled our bags to the brim and grabbed some food in 'Starbucks'. The milkshake I had went down a treat after a week of water warmed up by the sun.

What occurred next was one of the many situations where the good will of American people will never be forgotten. As we loaded our bags onto our backs, Ken being the talker that he is, struck up a conversation with a young couple ordering drinks. Within minutes he had them offering us a lift to Jim's house, so we didn't have to walk carrying the heavy bags. A big thank you to the couple that we then came to know as Andi and Ben.

Arriving back at Jim's, it was time to unload the kayaks, clean ourselves, our clothes, and our kit, before catching up with everyone back home and having a much-needed rest. I put together a quick video of the week for Facebook and the website and nodded off.

The night was spent relaxing, eating Fajitas and exchanging Mississippi headwater experiences with Jim, his wife Sharron, and their friends Brian and Judy. Brian was an ex-member of the RAF who many years earlier set a record for the quickest decent of the Mississippi (in other words he's madder than Ken and me). It was great to hear some of Brian and Jim's stories as they included advice about what was still to come, although I was sure they over exaggerated on some things just to make us worry.

I was more than thankful to have had a day off the river. I spent the last hour before bed dividing up the pile of snacks in my room into smaller bags for the remainder of the journey. At 10:30pm I was curled up in bed thinking of what lay ahead.

After a disrupted night's sleep, I was up early to finish my packing. After a hearty breakfast and a few hours later, we were in Jim's car on the way back to the river. The car journey gave me time to think...this was where the real adventure would start, up until then we had had the comfort of knowing we would be back at Jim's within the week. Now the only thing certain was that I had a flight leaving Louisiana on the 10th October which was around 2200 miles away! The adventure had just stepped up a notch.

As I pushed off from the bank, I waved goodbye to Jim. I will be eternally thankful to him and Sharron for their help and hospitality during the trip. After all, Ken and I were two strangers who they welcomed into their home with open arms, yet I felt as though I had known them all my life. I hoped that one day I would be able to go back there ... but certainly not by kayak!

Perhaps Ken too was feeling sentimental, perhaps we were contemplating our past week, and having thoughts of how we would now be paddling into the unknown, because at no point during the next 8 hours of paddling did we make real conversation; apart from the odd, 'let's have a snack' or, 'let's drift for 5', no words left our mouths.

We arrived 37 miles later (a new record) at our campsite for the night, 'Jacobson Campground' where we began the now familiar routine of erecting our tents and choosing between pasta, or rice and mash for tea. Whilst shopping previously we had bought a pack of 'Oreos' as a 'pick-me-up' on the harder days. Almost half the pack went that night!

On consulting the maps Ken announced that 40 miles was our target for tomorrow. My reaction was less than enthusiastic as I trudged off to my humble abode (aka my tent).

I was woken up at the now normal 6.30 am by Ken with the standard 'are you awake toots?' With camp packed up, I sat and consumed my daily bagel whilst being eaten alive by the swarms of mosquitoes attracted to my blood. This spurred me on, and I was back in my boat fast. iPod in…skeg down…gloves on…paddle left…paddle right…paddle left…paddle right…paddle left…paddle right…

Our friend the Bald Eagle was back as he swopped down in front of us as soon as we set off and led the way for most of the morning. 'Sandy Lake' was our aim for the day, a recreational campground that we hoped would have space for a couple of smelly Brits off the river, and thankfully it did. It was a long trek from the kayaks to our pitch, and with my shoulder still causing me pain, a slow process. We pitched our tents on our given spot, which should be pointed out was in fact for caravans and therefore mostly stone. Oh well, beggars can't be choosers. After changing clothes and applying my many creams, bite relief and Volterol, just to name two, I set to updating my journal…

'I hate insects

I hate Kayaking

I hate trees

I hate the Mississippi River

I hate this challenge

I hate paddling

I hate my shoulder

Another dull day!'

Saturday 16th August 2014. Sandy Lake.

Well, on reflection, I think that entry summed up the day well.

As we packed all our gear away and repeated the long journey to the boat ramp the next morning dark clouds began to gather above us. Ken shrugged off the idea of a storm and was adamant the clouds were heading away from us. They weren't, and just as we were leaving the boat ramp the heavens opened. I promptly banned Ken from commenting on the weather from now on. Strangely enough the rain improved my mood. The trees looked slightly different in the rain, a different shade of green and the day didn't seem quite as monotonous.

We had set ourselves a target of 20 miles that day and as the hours passed so did the miles. Late on in the day we stopped under a bridge to avoid another rainstorm and consult the map. According to Ken the town of Palisade (our spot for the night) and its campground was about 1 mile away. Prepared for another 15 minutes of paddling I pushed out into the rain. No sooner had my paddle contacted the water than I spotted a ramp to my right, which looked to lead to flat ground and some form of campsite.

"Is this it Ken?"

"It can't be we have only come 10 metres."

"Oh look, that sign says Pallisade, it must be."

It was. (Note to self, maps are to be sworn at not by)

Trying to keep ourselves and our kit as dry as possible we devised a make-shift shelter using the large tarpaulin we had brought and put our tents up underneath it. We then headed towards town in search of food. Pallisade, according to a sign as we approached, has a population of 167. We both began to doubt our chances of finding somewhere to eat. To our astonishment we discovered 2 petrol stations and 2 cafes, one of which was open, so we took refuge from the rain and ordered some hearty meals. The café had Wi-Fi, so all was well, and we stayed until closing time. We were both astounded to discover Andi and Ben (the helpful couple in Grand Rapids) had donated $200 to the Mississippi Challenge 2014. Suddenly the journey seemed a bit more achievable.

A storm was forecast again for the next day. Part of me prayed that it would come and that we wouldn't be able to paddle as my shoulder was getting worse by the day to the point that even lifting a fork to my mouth was agony.

We awoke the next morning and my prayers were answered. The predicted storm had arrived. Ken checked in with the weatherman on our radio. For all you 'West Yorkshire folk' he was no 'Paul, the Weatherman', instead his voice was as monotone as an answering machine. 'Mr monotone' informed us that storm was here to stay for the next few hours so we headed back to the café for breakfast as it would be pointless to even try and paddle in this weather, never mind having to pack away our soaking wet gear. Ken was suffering from back pain sustained whilst crossing Winnibigoshish and I still with my shoulder, so we made the joint decision to sit the storm out and then make our way down stream to the next camp a mere 8 miles away…not far but it would give our bodies the chance to recuperate and meant we would not have wasted a day.

A few hours later the rain eased off and we reluctantly trudged back to our camp. After packing away our rain-soaked kit and pulling on wet smelly clothes we began to idly paddle our way down river. With no pressure to stick to a certain speed we laughed and joked the miles away and soon arrived at the camp. Ken jumped out of his boat and went up the bank to scout the area; within seconds he had been bitten by several mosquitoes, apparently the campsite was infested with them, so we had a decision to make. Camp and face the bugs or paddle another 23 miles to the town of Aitken and the next possible campsite. We reluctantly chose to paddle, and as I put my headphones in my ears I very quickly sank back into the harsh reality of our current situation more pain, boredom and nothing much to look at but a brown river.

The rain fell on and off throughout the day as we covered the miles to Aitken, no sooner had we begun to dry off than the next shower of rain would hit us, and it continued like this all day. 23 miles extra completed we finally arrived at the campsite, no sooner had we pulled up onto the boat ramp than the biggest storm so far hit, and we had to run to the nearby toilets for shelter. From our position we could just see the river and boat ramp where we had left our kayaks and it was clear to see that the water was rising dramatically. As much as we both would have happily watched the kayaks float off down the river to render our challenge impossible to complete, we had to run out into the storm to rescue them.

Soaking wet, and with all our might, we pushed and pulled the kayaks up onto a mud banking to ensure they did not float away. As arduous work as it was, a moment of laughter broke the mood as Ken slipped down the banking and landed in a pile of mud. Resembling a pig in a mud bath, he then rolled around in the water that was gushing down the boat ramp to clean himself.

Assembling the tarpaulin once more we set up camp for the night. We misjudged the sizes of our tents slightly meaning I had to perform a matrix style movement through two tree trunks just to access my own front door but at least we were out of the rain. About an hour later we walked into town in the search of some food and we settled on Subway.

No sooner had we sat down than a group of men walked in each armed and in uniform. I wasn't too clued up on all the different branches of law enforcement in the States but after striking up a friendly conversation with them we learned that the group was made up of two Deputy Sheriffs, a State Trooper and a City Policeman. It also turned out that these 4 gentlemen made up the entire County Police night shift. I was amazed that so few people would cover such a big area.

After explaining what we were doing they offered us a lift back to our site, so being standard British tourists, we asked for a few pictures of us being shoved into the back of the car before getting on our way. Knowing the crime levels in the area they also offered to come round and check on us every couple of hours during the night, they were true to their word as I saw them drive past while struggling to sleep in the early hours of the morning.

I knew when I took on the challenge that one of the hardest points would be the sheer boredom of kayaking for 8-10 hours a day. The next day in particular would go down as one of the most tedious of them all.

Tuesday 19th August: the aim was to cover 40 miles and pitch for the night at 'Half Moon Campsite'. We awoke again to rain and the sound of thunder but thankfully (or not so thankfully) it soon cleared so we put too, and our daily routine began. Our clothes hadn't dried overnight so my underwear, t shirt and shorts were all freezing cold to put on, not a pleasant way to start the day.

I had both heard of and used the saying 'being bored to tears' many times in life but up until that day it had been just that, a saying. We paddled for hours on and on with little break, the scenery did not change and all we could see was just a brown river winding its way in front of us and two tall, tree lined banking's, no people and no wildlife and just silence. It was mind-numbing.

Even listening to my iPod or striking up ridiculous topics of conversation could not enthuse either of us on that day. With about an hour to go I heard Ken scream at the top of his lungs 'I'm bored'. It echoed on for miles down the long narrow channel of a river lined by towering trees. I felt exactly the same, the boredom was painful with nothing new to look at. Progress was slow and this allowed far too much time for negative thoughts to enter the mind. All I could think of was how this thing (the Whole Mississippi Challenge) was starting to seem more and more impossible. How was I going to maintain this for several more weeks? Thoughts of giving up and stopping plagued my brain as I tried to shut them out and focus on something else, anything else.

We hadn't even broken the '2000 miles to go' marker and each paddle stroke sent shooting pains through my shoulder, up my neck, and down my back. I was breaking both mentally and physically.

I think it says a lot about how boring the day was when the most interesting thing to happen was when I managed to have a pee without leaving my

Kayak. A lot of people during/before and after the challenge wanted to know how we did this, and not about the trip itself. What we saw, where we slept etc. No, it was "how did you go to the toilet". So, here you go.

In reality I didn't need to go to the loo too much on the river, perhaps we were just using up more water than we could take on, so I often found a tree or bush to hide behind on our lunch breaks, or if I did get caught short on river I would pull onto the banking and find somewhere to go. However, this would dramatically slow us down and as the river got wider even more so and as such, I had to find an alternative method.

Both Ken and I had a plastic porta loo canister for use during the night in our tents and I used this to be able to go to the loo while sat down in my boat, this was much faster than paddling to the shore. It involved combining the Shewee and porta pot with some good aiming with the funnel and delicate handling so that you didn't end up covered in your own wee. (I would like to just point out here that at no point did I end up dropping wee on myself). Business complete, you then disposed of the contents and carried on paddling. I actually became so skilled at this towards the end of the challenge that I wouldn't even have to worry about trying to stop my boat from moving.

That day was also a day that Ken and I both realised the true dangers of the river. As we were paddling along Ken opened his deck bag to get to his sun cream. Not realising he had left the flap open; his digital camera fell into the river. It remained afloat only for the length of time it took me to paddle over to it and sank instantly the moment I reached out to get it. I couldn't help but think how quick the river could suck in our kayaks if we ever got into difficulty. We needed another rule, Rule number 4 'never underestimate the strength of the river.'

We paddled on for hours and every minute spent on the river was making me feel worse. My eyes were stinging from the tears brought on simply through pain and boredom all I wanted was to get out of my boat and onto dryland. I had never wanted anything to end as much in my life and the thought of having to keep going for another few months made the tears fall faster. Every paddle stroke felt like I was being stabbed in the shoulder and there was nothing I could do to stop the pain other than wince and try to keep going.

Ken finally announced that we were only a few miles away from our camp, so I wiped away my tears of boredom and began to keep a look out. We arrived at the spot marked on the map to find the entrance completely blocked off. We paddled up a small backwater to try and gain access to it, but it was no use we could not get through the vegetation. Cue more tears.

Thankfully, a quick check of the map showed a boat ramp around the next bend, we decided to check that out and see if there would be some ground to camp on. We pulled up onto the ramp both exhausted and mentally drained. I could feel tears welling up again… this had been one of the worst days so far, there was no sign of any civilisation and the silence was deafening. I felt so alone, which was ironic really when Ken was only every a few metres away from me.

We put up our tents directly under a 'no camping' sign because we were clearly fearless. That and there was no other option. It was quite clear neither of us were getting back in our boats that day. I set too boiling water for our exquisite meal of dried mash and rice and headed to sleep. I wanted to get out of the reality of loneliness and boredom and into the safety of sleep as soon as possible.

'If I could just bottle the emotions I am feeling now, it would be so much more effective than trying to explain it, I hate this whole thing and I long to go home!'

Tuesday 19th August 2014. Half Moon Landing

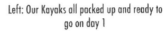

Left: Our Kayaks all packed up and ready to go on day 1

Right: At the official source of the river we each posed for a quick picture with a union flag

Left: The post signaling the official start point of the Mississippi River. It reads 'here 1475 ft above the ocean the mighty Mississippi begins to flow on its winding way 2552 miles to the Gulf of Mexico'

Right: The Mississippi resembles more of a stream than a river at it's early stages

Left: A couple of hours into day 1 and we were surrounded by vegitation, the only way to move forward was to dig your paddle into the reeeds or pull through with your hands.

Right: Our route was constantly blocked by trees and beever dams

Left: Pulling myself under a tree in the afternoon of day 2

Right: Our view from 'Pine Point' campsite and what we later called 'the green hell'. The river is somewhere in this shot.

Left: For the first week we kayaked along a river lined with vegitation, often much higher than us, which made it hard to navigate.

Right: As we approched Lake Bemiji we came across hundreds of people having a picnic and party on a sandbar half way across a lake.

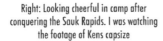

Left: Each night we would hang our food up in a tree away from our tents to keep the wild animals away form us as much as possible.

Right: Looking cheerful in camp after conquering the Sauk Rapids. I was watching the footage of Kens capsize

Left: With Sandy and her Mum after a breakfast stop of pancakes

Right: Sandy snapped a shot of us as we waved her goodbye

Left: Looking out across Lake Winnibigoshish at 13 miles wide it was impossible to see the far side.

Right: We became masters of packing a lot of gear into small spaces

Left: Resting and taking stock of our situation on a portage after having already crossed a car park.

Right: At the top of the flight of 50 steps which we had to carry both boats and all our equipment down

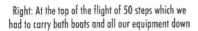

Left: Taking a moment after completing our longest and hardest portage

Right: Preparing to get out of our boats into what could only be described as a public pond, full of sludge and mud

Left: In Minnieapolis on a day off looking at the first of the locks that we would soon be facing as we progressed futher down river.

Right: The view from inside one of the locks

Left: Once below Minneapolis there was more river traffic to contend with. This is a picture of a relatively small barge

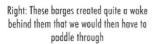
Right: These barges created quite a wake behind them that we would then have to paddle through

Left: Once inside the locks we had to hold onto a rope to keep us steady (this was often covered in spiders) and then wait to be lowered. This could take anywhere from 5-20 minutes

Right: The burns on my arms a few days after discovering them. You can just make out the large blisters on the right hand side

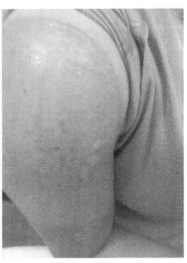

Left: After a couple of days off I was bandaged up and ready to paddle again.

Right: Being on the river before sunrise was a chance for me to air out my blisters as I rolled my shirt sleeves up. You can also see a barge in the background

CHAPTER 6
RIGHT PLACE, RIGHT TIME

To say my motivation was at an all-time low was an understatement as I woke the next morning. I dragged out my breakfast as much as I could, I was desperate to spend as much time off the river as possible. Ken summarised his psychological condition perfectly to me in a short conversation.

"Where are you heading?" I asked him as he walked with purpose away from me.

"Off to the toilet somewhere, I finally need to go... although I am tempted to just S*** in my kayak"

"So, then you have an excuse not to get back in it?"

"Yep"

I will quickly add, he did not go to the toilet in his Kayak, but the conversation made me chuckle even if I didn't feel joyful.

A point of interest here would be the effect we found that days of dehydrated meals had on our insides. Over the first week both Ken and I had realised we were needing to go to the toilet less and less and given we had exhausted most other conversations our talk soon turned to this, mostly out of interest as to whether the other was experiencing the same thing. It turned out we were so any time we actually managed to go to the loo was a cause for celebration and a topic of conversation.

Anyway, moving on from the toilet talk and back to the river...we had only been going a matter of minutes that day when we hit what is called a flood plain. These are large areas just before dams where water is held before it goes through. We came across a good number of them on our journey and they could start as much as around 7 miles away from the dam itself. They don't sound like too much a problem, but...stagnant water we learned means one thing. No flow.

While the natural flow of the river had been minimal up to this point (no more than 3mph) this had still allowed us to maintain a pace of around 6 miles an hour on average throughout the day. However, once we hit a flood plain and the flow vanished our travel speed would be slashed as we could only move on our own power.

Floor plains were demanding work and made it feel more like we were paddling through treacle than the 4th longest river in the world. In fact, we often made such slow progress across them that the GPS refused to accept that we were even moving.

We had decided back in Grand Rapids after some advice from Jim that we would set a pattern to our mileage, 2 days hard slog up in the 30 miles+ area, and one shorter day at about 15 miles. This would help us to slowly prepare our bodies for the multiple-mile days we would have to complete later in the journey. This day was one of the shorter ones and we arrived at our destination early afternoon, a campsite at a country park on the North side of the city of Brainerd. Our spirits were lifted at the thought of a good bit of R and R.

Now I am sure everyone reading this, just like Ken and I, would expect a 'campsite' to accommodate all types of guests. Caravans, Tents etc. However, this 'campsite' did not allow tents.

Cue a confused and frustrated looking pair of Brits!

Anger at the situation soon took over me and I went to sit down on a nearby wall just to keep myself calm. My body was aching severely, my shoulder was throbbing, and I just needed to be out of my kayak. I had thought our day was over...instead we would now have to paddle back across the flood plain, around the town, and then once there a further 3 miles to the next possible campsite.

Maps showed this as a marked Country Park just like the one we were currently in, so we did not hold out much hope of being able to camp there either. Instead, it was likely we would have to cover another 15 miles to a spot marked by the DNR as a campsite. Our 'short 15 miles day' was now looking more like another 30+.

Incredibly frustrated at the whole situation we reluctantly got back into our boats and set off back through the treacle. To help split the now longer day for us, we decided to stop at the bottom side of town to get some good food in us as the camp sites further down river didn't look to be near civilisation according to the map.

As we pulled ashore and climbed the banking, we realised we were on the outskirts of another park. Ken persuaded some passers-by to take pity on us and give him a lift into town to a sandwich shop. I stayed to guard the kayaks and made conversation with a few locals about our journey. After a while Ken returned with fresh sandwiches and we ate in silence, too exhausted to speak. Before too long it was time to get going again and I began to prepare myself and my kayak for the last slog of the day.

As I began to push my boat out into the water my leg suddenly sunk quickly down into the mud, I tugged my foot free, broke my shoe in the process and now covered in mud I scrambled back into my boat.

Thankfully the rest of the day passed quickly, helped along by the river slightly as the flow picked up and we reached record speed of 7.6 mph. Our spirits were lifted, and conversation was flowing so much so that we almost paddled straight past our camping spot due to talking too much.

I pulled ashore and went ahead to scout the camp site. It was a long walk of about half a mile down a small winding path on the river's edge. (I much preferred the view of it when not on it.) I entered a clearing to discover many RV's and tents and what looked very much like a well organised fee-paying campsite. I explained what I had seen to Ken and we decided because it was quite a trek with our equipment that we would camp near the boat ramp instead. This time above the sign saying, 'no camping', we were becoming quite the rebel campers.

I do not know whether it was waking up to a thunderstorm and knowing we were going nowhere fast or the fact that we were finally under the 2000 miles to go marker, but I woke the next day feeling refreshed and motivated to get going again. This new wave of motivation lasted about 5 minutes on the water and I was soon bored.

This state of mind was with me for most of the week. To keep myself going I had to break down my days into smaller chunks and portages (carrying the kayaks around an obstacle) helped to do this. As tiring as they were, it meant some time out of my kayak and off the river. Little did we know that the portages were only going to get harder and less kayak friendly.

It was just another average day on the river when we arrived at Blanchard Dam. We had heard horror stories about this portage… "it's the worst portage on the Mississippi, if you can avoid it do so at all costs". Anyone could be fooled into thinking that as these portages had been created and marked by people no different to us that some consideration about placement may have been considered. It became clear to Ken and I at this Dam that this was not the case in the slightest.

We pulled up, at the bottom of a steep slope next to the portage sign, in water covered in so much debris and wild plant life that it resembled more a pond in a community park than the mighty Mississippi River. One look at each other was enough to say we did not particularly want to get out into it but we didn't really have any other option. I reached for my Neoprene Socks (at least then I would not have to feel anything) and started the arduous task of putting them on in my kayak. Ken was out of his boat before me and went ahead to scout the route.

Back in Grand Rapids, Jim Lewis had given us the number of a man called John who had helped him and his companions out at this dam when he had done the same trip. Ken had been trying to contact him on and off throughout the day but to no avail. Of course, as soon as Ken was out of ear shot his phone began ringing. However, I was still floating around in the gunk struggling to get my socks on and could not get to Ken's boat to reach into the deck bag to grab his phone. It rang a further 3 times but each time it was impossible for me to reach it. Finally, after what felt like an hour Ken returned but he was not alone.

One of the many things Ken is particularly good at is talking to people and somehow getting them to want to help us, but this occurrence of strangers being helpful must be the biggest coincidence I have ever experienced in my life. Ken told me the story as this….

"I was walking along the portage path for what felt like miles, I could not even see the river. A man was approaching me with a fishing rod, so I jokingly said if you're fishing there must be a river nearby. The stranger replied, "yes its maybe a couple of blocks in that direction" (how far is a block in the woods?). So, on I went in the direction he had pointed. A few minutes later I heard the pattering of feet behind me, of course I assumed the worst and thought the man was coming back to kill me. Instead, he asked, "with an accent like that can I ask you something. Do you know Jim Lewis?""

So, Ken's murderer was in fact a man named Bob White who had randomly met Jim a month back whilst out kayaking. They had got into talking about the two crazy Brits Jim would be helping to start off their journey down the Mississippi in a month's time, and when he had heard Ken's British accent he had put two and two together and realised Ken must be one of said crazy Brits'.

I don't know if I will ever be able to decide what I was more thankful for in that crazy situation, to Jim who had just happened to strike up a conversation with a stranger a month back, to Ken who had decided to crack a joke just at the right moment, or that John had not answered his phone (because if he had we wouldn't have bothered going to check out the route and therefore not met Bob). But each of these strange occurrences lead to us now having a helping hand for the portage. I explained to Ken that his phone had been ringing, he checked to see if it was John, it was, and he would be bringing a trailer in half an hour to help us around the dam.

With help on the way we thanked Bob for his generous offer of help and then said our goodbyes as he packed up his gear to head off home to Minneapolis and we paddled back upriver to a boat landing where John was to meet us. I took the chance to phone home whilst we waited for our lift; my Great Aunties would be at my house meaning I could talk to them for the first time since I set off. Whilst on the phone I saw Bob return and talk to Ken. Once off the phone I discovered he had offered us his house for the night once we reached Minneapolis as well as a sightseeing tour as he would hopefully have the day off work, if we timed it right. Hallelujah! A day off and a shower was in sight!

John arrived to help us with the portage and went the 'extra mile' by taking us to Walmart to stock up on supplies. Jim Lewis had saved us again. We finished the day uplifted, knowing we were finally near to Minneapolis (the place we had flown into nearly two weeks ago) and would be able to have a day off with Bob. We found a picturesque campsite to stop at, overlooking...yes you guessed it... the river of course.

CHAPTER 7
I GET KNOCKED DOWN; I GET UP AGAIN

In the run up to Minneapolis we encountered some of the worst portages of the whole trip, miles long, along the sides of main roads, up pebbled hills and across car parks, you name it we did it.

One particular day consisted of two long portages and a set of rapids and these will go down in my history as the portages from hell.

After kayaking all morning and negotiation the flood plain, we pulled up at 'Sartell Dam' on the North side of the city of the same name. We followed our usual procedure of tracking to the banking several hundred of meters away from the dam itself and pulled ourselves ashore. Ken took the turn of scouting the route on this one and came back a while later to say he had turned back before had had even come across the put in point, the walk had been that long.

We heaved our boats out of the water and dug out our wheels, this was going to be a long walk. We attached a sling each to the front of our boats so we could at least rest some of the weight on our shoulders instead of bending down constantly to hold the handle on the bow.

Off we went down the main road that ran parallel to the river pulling the boats along behind us. I was feeling physically stronger now after all the days of kayaking and once moving felt quite comfortable pulling 90kg along. However, after about 0.5 mile my strength was waning, and I was having to stop regularly to switch the shoulder which I had the sling on. My bad shoulder was struggling to take the weight but with that being my dominant arm I didn't feel as comfortable with it on my other arm. Ken wasn't fairing much better as he was having a lot of trouble with his wheels meaning he was probably supporting around 75% of the weight on his shoulders. It was a hard walk and by the time we found our put in point, a mile later, we were exhausted.

We didn't have much time to rest as we knew we had another portage coming up in a matter of miles but before that we had an even bigger obstacle, rapids.

Sauk Rapids was another of those parts of the river that we had heard a lot about, treacherous when the river is running high and impassable if it is low. At about 200 metres long they are classed as Grade 1 rapids (in kayaking rapids are classified into numbers, 1 being the easiest and 5+ being insane) so they weren't going to be crazy currents and whirlpools, but they would provide challenge for us as still somewhat inexperienced paddlers.

Being a bit of an adrenaline junky I had been looking forward to these from day 1, Ken wasn't quite as enthusiastic and given the chance I think he would have avoided them completely by portaging around. Given the stories we had heard about them we decided we would get nearer and then make our decision as to whether they were safe to negotiate.

A great idea but rendered impossible as by the time we got close enough to hear them the banks were too steep to stop or get out, we had no option but to go down them.

Without paddling my pace suddenly increased as I was caught up in the fast current heading for the first section of the rapids. I sat up tall braced my feet onto the foot holds in my kayak and gripped my paddles as I sped up towards the white caps.

I let out a cry of joy as I smashed into the first wave and felt the water splash onto my face. It was great fun; I was moving fast but felt to be in control as my boat reacted to my every paddle stroke with precision. They may have only been rapids of the lowest class but the white water splashing in my face, my stomach being turned by the swells, and the sheer increase in speed, created a great adrenaline rush. I felt in control and all was going well, I was on rapids for the first time and I was holding my own.

I turned around to check on Ken. Whenever I was ahead, I would make a point of checking behind me every few minutes to ensure all was well, and on the rapids, this was no different.

He let out a whistle and we carried on paddling our way over the swells.

I will never know what made me look around the next time, as I had only checked on Ken a matter of seconds ago, but I did. That's when I saw the back of his boat swing out behind him and almost as if in slow motion, capsize, taking Ken straight under the swell of the cresting waves.

I instantly about turned and began battling against the current and waves to get to him as quick as possible. My mind was in overdrive thinking through our training and what I could do to help and get Ken upright again. What if I couldn't get to him in time? What if he couldn't get out of his boat?

During our capsize training we had been taught that if one boat was upturned the other person had to simply ram the bow of their boat into the side of the upturned one, and the person underneath the water would grab hold and pull themselves up. This works great in a swimming pool, but I was not sure about on rapids where it could take minutes to get to the other person.

I was paddling as fast as I could whilst my mind filtered through ideas of what to do but it was incredibly hard to move anywhere fast as the current was so strong. For every two strokes I did I travelled back half the way I had come. My heart was racing.

Suddenly I saw Ken emerge from underneath his boat…he was safe…for now.

I unhooked the throwline from my boat, and once I got close to Ken, I clipped myself on to his kayak whilst shouting out to tell him to stay in contact with it so I could pull him ashore safely. I set off across the current to the shore about 50 metres away. I heard Ken shout to me and turned to see he could now touch the bottom. Moments later he scrambled onto shore and we both let out a sigh of relief, shortly followed by howls of laughter. Well, when it's a laugh or cry situation, laughing is a much more enjoyable option.

Ken surveyed his kayak and equipment and was astounded to find he had not lost a single thing. This for Ken, the person who had already lost two hats, a camera, a pair of glasses and a water bottle, was an incredible feat. While bailing out his kayak we swapped stories of the event and were on our way once more about half an hour later. Wow that was eventful! I felt a deep sense of pride for both of us as we paddled on. We had made it through our first experience on rapids, yes one of us did capsize, but we had remained calm, trusted each other and got ourselves out of the situation safely. I chuckled to myself as after all an event like that makes for great story telling, even if Ken had now broken Rule number 1.

Next up in our day of challenges was St Cloud Hydro Dam, if our portage earlier in the day had been hard it was nothing up to this one. I ran ahead to scout and soon saw what lay ahead, I returned to break the news to Ken, it was going to be another long one.

We repeated the process from earlier and fixed our wheels onto both boats and began what would be the hardest portage of the whole trip. Even more upsetting was the fact that we were running out of water and there was a place for topping up on fresh water next to our takeout point. Having not seen anything further down the path we had no option but to fill up all our bottles there, meaning more weight to carry for the portage.

Stocked up on water the first thing we had to do was walk through a busy car park avoiding reversing vehicles and children running all over, next was an uphill climb through a park where people were playing disc golf. If this wasn't enough, we then had to descend a winding set of 50 steps no wider than the boats themselves to get back to the river. We stopped at the top of the steps and 'gutted' the boats of water, deck bags and anything easily removable to minimise the weight and then proceeded to carry the boats one at a time down the steps. As I grabbed OLLI (Kens Kayak) I let out a cry and dropped it as I felt a shooting pain go straight from my shoulder to my neck, this was going to be painful. I gritted my teeth as I picked up OLLI once more and began to descend the steps. 6 times we went up and down the steps to get both boats and all our gear down.

Once the portage was complete, I dropped my boat and walked to the water's edge exhausted. I soon concluded that whoever designed the portage routes must have never been in a boat in their life. If they had, they would have known that trying to carry a fully loaded kayak, weighing about 90kg, several miles, down a flight of winding steps no wider than the boat itself was nigh on impossible. I was certainly starting to feel stronger from the constant physical exercise, but I still believed that even some of the strongest men in the world would have labelled this as a challenge. Note to Mr or Mrs Portage Surveyor on the Mississippi: I am not your biggest fan.

That night we found a quite site just off to the left-hand side of the river, which was raised up slightly on flat ground, it even had a picnic bench. Tents up and food cooked we decided it was time to review the footage from our cameras from our adventures in the rapids. Both Ken and I had a waterproof camera each attached to our boats at all times and had made sure to press record before descending the rapids. We spent the evening chuckling at each other's footage from the capsize, Ken's camera facing the water showed his boat slowly tip over and into the water, my camera; facing me had caught the sheer look of panic and minor swear words as I had seen Ken be consumed by the water. We slept well after our eventful and physically challenging day.

We were now gaining on Minneapolis and knew we would be there in a matter of days. My focus was now to make it there; the place we had flown into meaning from then on, I would be heading further south than I had ever been. I don't know whether it was this outlook that spurred me on the next morning, but I was 'in the zone' and could have paddled for hours without complaining.

Most days I had to constantly keep my mind occupied through either talking or playing games to avoid negative thoughts. Therefore, it was a strange occurrence to have a day when my mind was simply blank, my head was down, I could just paddle on for hours as I was in my own world and was quite happy. This next day was one of those days.

As we paddled along Ken pulled alongside me eager for conversation, I could tell he was having a bad day, so I thought of a topic (the alphabet game) and he played along. Game finished, boredom suddenly hit me again and I felt down.

Both feeling quite down we decided to treat ourselves for lunch. A quick consultation of Google maps showed there to be a Domino's Pizza place not far down the road of where we had pulled up. Result! As normal, I stayed with the boats and Ken went on the pizza run. He came back around half an hour later but wasn't alone or on foot, he had managed to persuade the staff at the shop to deliver both the pizzas and him back to the river, only Ken could get away with that.

Pizzas devoured we were on our way again; we had no planned stopping point for the day so once we had hit our milage goal we began to look out for somewhere to call a camp site for the night.

A park was shown on the map to the right of the river and when we reached it. I jumped ashore to scout it out. On my return I explained to Ken how we seemed to have pulled up at a County Park teeming with people and that I wasn't sure we would be able to stop there. I suggested I head further down the path to see what I could find.

I started to jog away from Ken towards the bottom end of the park, however after spending 8 hours sat down in a Kayak, jogging was not easy. My legs felt like jelly and my knees kept giving way underneath me, I must have looked like a young child walking for the first time. I passed through a large area of trees and found a small but steep sand bank on my left running down to the river. There was a small patch of grass at the top hidden behind bushes that I thought may do as a discrete campsite.

I headed back to Ken passing what looked to be a wedding party and told him what I had found. We paddled further down to the sand bank pulled ashore and set up camp. A few minutes later I got sudden stabbing pains in my stomach something was telling me the Domino's pizza had been a bad idea. Perhaps eating such rich food after weeks of dehydrated meals doesn't do good things to your digestive system. I needed to find a loo and quickly but there wasn't one in sight…great, a bush would have to do. Once the toilet situation was sorted, it was then time for a wash in the river. (You know you smell bad when you can smell yourself). We spent the night relaxing and watching the world go by, at one point we thought we may get asked to leave as a member of staff came by on a grass cutter, but he didn't even bat an eye lid. Our spirits were high, we only had one more day of kayaking before we would arrive in Minneapolis.

We broke camp early the next day and after a long morning's paddle through yet more 'treacle' and dams we finally pulled up at the top side of the city of Minneapolis and met Bob who was waiting for us with his truck. Happy to be off the river and with a day off on the cards we strapped our boats to the roof and happily jumped in the van for our drive through the city.

Not having seen much of Minneapolis on my arrival it was great to get my first taste of an American city and it was just like you see on the TV, high rise towers interspersed with the occasional parks or grass land. We were soon out into the suburbs, where the long roads were now lined with houses with immaculate lawns. It seemed a really nice place.

As we pulled up outside Bob's house, we heard the start-up of a motor, it was incredibly loud and drew our attention. It turned out it was nothing exciting, only a man on a sit on lawn mower tidying up his 3 x 3 metre square garden. I thought a sit on mower seemed a bit excessive for something so small, but each to their own.

Eager to make the most of our down time we set too on washing our clothes and giving the kayaks a good clean out, after several days of us sitting in them they smelt of sweat, were covered in mud and littered with all kinds of river debris and food. After that it was time for a shower, our first in over a week. As I scrubbed my skin the water turned brown as it trickled off me and into the plug hole, it took a good 20 minutes to get somewhat clean but oh boy, it felt good.

I made a few calls and skyped friends back home before uploading more videos to social media, this took most of the day and then it was time for a BBQ. Bob and his wife laid on a fantastic spread as we relaxed out in their garden, burgers, sausages and all manner of different food was available to us. A moment of humour occurred as Ken went back into the house to help himself to the last burger, to find it was no longer there, one of Bob's dog suddenly looked a bit shifty in the corner.

That evening Ken and Bob were busy looking at the maps and discussing the rest of our journey. I stayed out of this, even the thought of looking at a map made my stomach turn…we still had so far to go.

The next day was spent looking around Minneapolis and was a welcome break from the river. It felt great to be walking and stretching my legs. We paid a quick visit to an outdoor shop that had a massive selection of guns, given this isn't something you see in England we spent some time looking and even managed to persuade the staff member to allow me to hold one. He and Ken decided to have me hold a pink camouflage one as we snapped a quick picture.

Next up on our hit list was a visit to the river itself to look at the first 2 of the 28 locks that we would now be facing. Up until this point any dams or obstacle had required us to portage round them, from now on we would be able to use the locks as the law states anyone whether in a barge, pleasure craft, or a simple kayak, must be allowed passage through.

These locks would range in a drop height from 1 foot (0.3 metres) to 40 feet (12 metres) and it would take us just short of 3 weeks to pass through them all.

We arrived at St Antony Falls and the sight of the first 2 locks. You know something is going to be quite big when there is a visitor centre attached to it. Big it was, and as we stood on the bridge above the gushing water we were watching people seemingly the size of ants walking up and down the stone walls.

We finished our tour at a museum where me and Ken wasted sometime while waiting for Bob to finish a work call before heading back. As was now the norm we called in at a Walmart to top on our supplies and I spent the rest of the day sorting these out. As night drew in, I could feel a sense of dread building up, I really wasn't feeling enthusiastic to get back on the river. A day off had meant a day without shoulder pain and I wasn't looking forward to this returning the next day.

PART 4:
MINNEAPOLIS TO ST LOUIS

'Strength does not come from winning. Your struggles develop your strength. When you go through hardship and decide not to surrender that is strength' Arnold Schwarzenegger

CHAPTER 8
LOCK LOCK, WHO'S THERE

Well, here we go again, back to it, it's time to paddle, my state of mind I would say is neutral, again I am just counting days not miles. Whether we complete this river or not I am flying home on 10th October!

Wednesday 27th August 2014. Red Wing

I awoke filled with dread; it was time to paddle again.

Bob drove us back to the river and we began the long but now perfected process of repacking our kayaks ready to continue our journey. As we laid all our gear out on the boat ramp Bob said…

'There is no way you are getting all that in your boats'

He looked on in awe as each bit went into its spot and the boat ramp emptied.

It was soon time to say goodbye and thank you to Bob as we pushed off from the edge of the bank and back onto the river.

We hadn't paddled more than a few meters before we met our new river friends who would be with us now for the remainder of our journey. Mississippi Barges.

At 200 feet (60.9 meters) long and around 35 feet (10.6 metres) wide, the barges were huge and at first a pretty terrifying sight. Used to transport coal, grain and all other types of materials up and down America, the furthest they could travel upriver was Minneapolis and they would use the lock system to make their way down to the Gulf of Mexico for their goods to be shipped off to foreign destinations. The Mississippi River had started as a small stream it was very quickly turning into something resembling a highway.

As the first barge approached us, we paddled away and across to the bank aiming to stay as far away as possible. As it chugged past us, we saw the tow boat at the back where the pilot was and as he waved merrily at us, we got hit by the wake. Water was gushing from the back of the tow and that combined with the sheer size of the containers created a large v shaped set of waves to be sent out across the width of the river and cause whatever it encountered to be thrown around, especially Kayaks. We were still bouncing around on the waves minutes after the barge had passed us.

As we paddled on, we became more comfortable with the barges and what to do in their presence. Basically, get out of the way as the chance of the pilot being able to see us if we were in front of them was very small.

Barges were the reason for the locks needing to be on the river and not long into our day it was time to go through our first one.

As we approached Ken radioed ahead to warn them that we were on our way and to ask what the procedure was. The man on the other end of the radio advised us that as they were currently in the process of bringing another boat up so there would be a 20-minute wait. It could have been worse!

We pulled up on a nearby sandbar to wait. I was excited to go through the locks, the same couldn't be said for Ken, but anything that broke the monotony of paddling all day was welcomed by me.

Finally, the time came, and we were summoned forward by the man on the radio. The lock was huge, at least over 100 meters long with walls towering above us on both sides. The gates shut behind us silently and we waited to be told what to do.

"Head right down the other end there's some ropes to hold onto" came a call from above

Off we went to find the ropes, which turned out to be covered in spiders and all manner of creepy crawlies. Yuck! To say such a large volume of water was being moved around us the entire process was very quiet and at points hard to work out if we were even moving. We sat quietly not wanting to miss any information being shouted down to us, but there was none, and we just sat there unsure what to do.

Around 20 minutes later I jumped out of my skin as a loud horn blasted out across the air.

It turned out that was a signal for us to get going and the gates in front of us suddenly started to open in a somewhat ominous way. It reminded me of when the 'Black Gates of Mordor' are opened in Lord of the Rings. We paddled our way out of the lock and back onto the usual surroundings of brown underneath and green all around.

A few hundred meters clear of the lock Ken shouted out.

"I have news", he had a huge grin on his face. "That's Wisconsin" as he pointed to the left bank of the river.

Finally, after 20 days in Minnesota we had made it into another state. Such was our excitement that we paddled over and up onto the bank. I think my exact words were "WE'RE IN WISCONSIN! Bog off Minnesota". I was too busy celebrating to realise how far up onto the bank I had gone, and it took me a good, few minutes to shuffle free of the sand and back onto the water.

It felt like we were finally making progress having made it to another state. Our spirits were high for the rest of the day, the sun was shining, and we were making good process. Not to mention, we had accumulated a huge 500 miles paddled. Never did I think I would ever paddle 500 miles in my life.

We decided on Red Wing as our spot to camp for the night and on arrival we pulled up at a dock and headed to the nearest bar aptly named the 'Harbour Bar'. The great food and great service was just what we needed.

That night would not go down as the best on the river for Ken. We were situated on another RV only site which the owner had kindly allowed us to stay on, however we were next to a fish cutting hut and toilets (resulting in some questionable smells), underneath a highway, and opposite a train yard, all equalling a noisy night or, so Ken said, I slept through it all. I must have been tired!

Even though I'd had a good night's sleep it did nothing to help me get through the trials and tribulations of the next day. As we left the campsite at Red Wing, we made our way to the next lake we would have to cross, Lake Pepin. At 25 miles long and at times only 3 feet deep it was going to be a challenge.

A challenge it was. As soon as we turned around the bend in the river to begin our crossing we were hit with an incredibly strong headwind. A quick look at our wind speed counter told us we were fighting against a 20mph block of wind that would likely stay with us the whole way across Lake Peppin. 20mph may not sound horrendous but when in a small boat moving only by the strength of your paddle strokes, its hard work.

We tried to paddled forwards making next to no progress. At one point even, the GPS registered us as travelling backwards. It was demanding work and was most likely going to get worse. If I wasn't striking the floor with each paddle stroke, I was being sprayed in the face by the water. We tracked off away from the riverbank hoping to find deeper water and tried to keep a watchful eye for barge traffic and of course it was at this point that my body decided I need the loo. Trying to pee into a porta pot while being bounced up and down and splashed in the face by waves was hard work and I would not recommend it.

Our aim for the day was to reach the town of Pepin about 25 miles away. We continued on making very little progress and to add to our troubles fog was moving towards us across the water and visibility was getting worse by the second. The day felt to be slowly becoming impossible. I put my head in my hands for a moment to try and give myself a pep talk and find some small piece of motivation, but it was impossible, I simply let out a groan and we continued our long slog across the lake.

Moments later I turned to see Ken had suddenly disappeared. I scanned the riverbank over half a mile away and could just make out his yellow Kayak. How had we managed to get so far apart? My only explanation was because I'd had my head down, (as had he) turning away from the wind and spray whilst paddling, I had completely missed him veering off to the left bank. I heard him shout something but couldn't make out what. I looked ahead to try and work out what he could be saying and there was my answer, on the right bank about 2 miles away was a town.

I waved my hands around in the general direction of the town and tried to shout across to him

"we are heading there instead, yeh?"

Ken waved his arms back at me and I soon realised he was telling me to paddle across to him. I waved my arms back in a 'no I'm heading that way' motion (whatever that was) but it must have worked. In my own defence I wasn't being argumentative or lazy in anyway but to me it seemed pointless when I was heading in a straight line towards the town, to turn my boat around and paddle the half mile across to the other bank to then have to paddle back across and then to the town, that just didn't make any sense. I was low on energy and this just seemed a silly way to use it. Instead, I slowly made progress as Ken paddled nearer to me.

We could see dark rain clouds ahead; a major storm was brewing, and it was coming quickly. Having no wish to be caught up in it, we needed to find somewhere to take shelter and quick. As we approached the town we pulled up on a beach below a bunch of houses and asked one of the owners if she could keep an eye on our boats while we sought refuge in the town. She agreed.

After much walking around, we found a room for the night and were informed of a car park we could use... (I would have thought it obvious we hadn't arrived by car with buoyancy aids and splash skirts on, but apparently not). We also discovered a small beach area further round from where we had left our boats and closer to our hotel. So, we headed back, completed the small but horrendous paddle to the other beach and proceeded to unload our kayaks.

We secured out boats in a parking space next to the hotel (after all they said we could use it) and checked in. We always loved the moment during check in when we were asked for vehicle descriptions and registration plates and could answer with Red and Yellow kayak.

It was at this hotel that our next major problem would arise...

CHAPTER 9
THE SUN HAS GOT HIS HAT ON

'Just as I thought things were looking up, Mother Nature and the river hit me in the face…literally'.

Thursday 28th August 2014. Lake City

"Ken…this doesn't look good, look at my arm."

Oh dear, would be the polite way to phrase his reply.

Having checked into our hotel room, I had hopped in the shower as normal to find that as soon as any water touched my arms they started stinging. I looked in the mirror to see that the top of my right shoulder down to the top half of my bicep was red raw and covered with large yellow blisters, some solid, some weeping. I looked in horror at my arm wondering what on earth I had done. Finishing up my shower it was at this point that I went to find Ken.

"I just spotted them as I grabbed a shower, they are incredibly sore, I couldn't let water go on them."

"What about your other arm?"

Not even thinking about my other arm I looked to see that there was also a smaller number of blisters in the same place on my left arm. (Safe to say I won't repeat what came out of my mouth at that moment)

After much deliberation and consulting of Google we settled on the fact that I had severe sunburn (2nd degree to be exact) and it must have happened the previous day when it had been incredibly hot. I filled with dread, had I just destroyed my chances of making it to the end of the journey?

I had been aware a few days prior of the sun feeling hot on my arms but had kept applying my factor 75(+) sun cream every few hours to try and limit and damage, so I was not expecting this reaction. I had never had problems with burning in the past and my shoulders had only been exposed for a few hours.

It was safe to say that me getting burnt was going to cause us problems. I knew from the fact that the pain was getting worse by the minute that there was no way I was going to be able to paddle the next day and maybe even the one after that. I needed some medical help and quickly if we were to have any chance of getting going again soon.

Help did arrive but not in the way we expected.

As we both sat feeling incredibly down about the whole situation and worried about my arms, we switched on the TV to see the weather channel. The presenter did nothing to lift our spirits by informing us that the storm we had seen coming in across the lake earlier that day would set in and last the whole next day. We were going nowhere. As frustrating as this was, we decided to be optimistic at least we would now have chance for my arms to recover.

A few days before these events a man named John Sullivan had been in contact asking us to get in touch when we were close to La Crosse, his hometown. John was part of a group of people known as 'River Angels'; members of the community who live local to the Mississippi and volunteer their hospitality to people traveling along it. That explanation does not do them justice at all, but I hope my story telling will paint a better picture.

Ken contacted John and explained our situation. He had been following our progress via GPS. He was concerned for our safety in the weather and was glad we had called him. Before we could even say 'thank you' he said he would be at the hotel tomorrow to take us to his house where we would sit out the storm. With that side of our problem sorted (thanks once again to the kindness of Americans), we now had the small matter of my burns and how to treat them, so I could at least rest comfortably. Racking our brains and Google for quick treatments led us to conclude that simply trying to keep them clean and covered for now would have to do until we could find ointment of some form. Ken rushed out to the local petrol station to try and find some form of bandaging whilst I phoned home to break the news to my parents. They offered me a few treatment ideas and tried their best to cheer me up.

We found a loose bandage that provided some relief to my arms and then ventured out into the rain for some food. Burger King was our only option, so we had both lunch and dinner there. At least all the kayaking would help burn off the calories.

It was a restless night due to the pain from my arms, a side sleeper most of the time having to lay on my back with constant throbbing in my arms was uncomfortable and I got very little sleep. Even more frustratingly we awoke the next morning to the sun shining across Lake Pepin. So much for the predicted storm.

However, I had been right in thinking I would be unable to paddle, just sitting up in bed or moving my arms the tiniest bit was agony, so storm or no storm, we were going nowhere.

I removed the bandages to try and get some air to the blisters and was shocked to see they had grown bigger in size and were now looking even more vicious, finding something to treat them with was becoming more urgent by the minute.

After breakfast John arrived to take us to his house in La Crosse. He and Ken loaded the kayaks onto his roof as I sat and watched the world go by, feeling useless with my arms limited to being stuck by my side. On the way we called at a local pharmacy, where unlike those in the UK they actual have booths where you can talk to a professional, show them your injuries, and they will tell you what you need. You then locate it on the shelves and buy it at the checkout. I was advised to purchase a number of creams and was given a formidable choice...

"This one will sting horrendously when you apply it but will cure the burns faster, whereas this one, will be more soothing but may take a bit longer to heal them... "

Well, they say no pain - no gain, so we bought the quickest working cream and were on our way again. 2 hours and a quick nap later we pulled up at John's house, another beautifully situated house in the suburbs of the city.

Once inside it was time to get the first lot of cream on my arms. Anyone within the vicinity of John's house must have wondered what was going on as I cried out in pain when Ken began to apply the cream. Wow, it stung.

That evening John insisted he took us out to a local restaurant and we eventually settled on one next to the river. The waitress asked if we would like a table with a river view and seemed shocked when Ken and I answer together with a firm 'no'. I had seen enough of it to last me a lifetime already. The topic soon turned to the next day's paddling, where we would put in, how far we would go, and what time we would set off. I listened and tried to keep expectations realistic, my arms hurt at the slightest movement.

Throughout the day some of the blisters had burst only to come back bigger and more vicious. I was in agony. I knew in my heart of hearts I wouldn't be able to paddle the next day, but I have always been one to believe it's never over till it's over, so I would pray for a miracle and see how I felt in the morning.

It seemed ironic that all I had really wanted before this situation was to go home and stop this trip, but now there was a realistic possibility of this happening I just wanted to keep going. Perhaps the amount of pain I was in 'top trumped' all the suffering on the river, but whatever it was, I was certainly a mixed bag of emotions.

Considering my physical condition, I had a peaceful night's sleep and woke up at my regular time of 6 am. As I lay in my bed trying to recall what I was doing and where I was, I heard Ken and John talking downstairs. It wasn't until I tried to get out of bed and couldn't move my arms that it all came flooding back to me. I took one look at the bandages and could see they had been weeping throughout the night and were stained yellow. I would have to change them before I did anything else.

I removed them as gently as possible, pulling off skin and watching the blisters burst as I gritted my teeth, eyes watering. All I wanted to do was scream out in pain, as I applied cream to the fresh raw skin.

I thought back to the days when I used to go to swimming lessons as a child and remembered how before one session, I had badly grazed my knee at school (no doubt I had tried to swing from a tree or something similar). I can remember crying all the way to the swimming pool as I was scared because I knew the chlorine in the water would make the graze sting. It took an age for my teacher to coax me into the pool. It seemed laughable when I looked at the situation I was in now. What I would give to be back at the swimming pool dealing with a simple graze.

After managing to dress myself I wandered down into the kitchen where Ken was already in his paddling gear with his kit piled at the door and was ready to go. One look at his hopeful face and I burst into tears, I tried to talk but I couldn't, I felt I had let him, and everyone down. I just stood there head down tears falling to the floor.

It seemed no words of explanation were needed for John. He knew we were going nowhere and within minutes he had removed our kayaks from the roof of his car and was making arrangements for us to stay another night.

Unbeknown to us up until that point, his family were visiting for the weekend and were due to be sleeping in the beds we had slept in. As much as Ken tried to persuade him to take us to a hotel so as we didn't impede upon his family time, he would have none of it. We would be staying another night and that was it. Again, someone unknown to us before undertaking this adventure, who had simply got in touch via a Facebook group, was saving us in a time of need. John and his wife Beth truly deserved the title of 'River Angels'.

That day I tried to relax as much as possible and to enjoy my day off by catching up with Phil, my Mum, Dad and Brother. It was a good pick me up. I spent some time looking at Google Maps, noting how far we had already travelled, and a sense of pride came over me. 500 plus miles was no mean feat, even if I had been an idiot and got myself sunburnt. The day passed quickly, and it was soon time for bed, a disrupted night ended when I awoke at 4 am and couldn't get back to sleep. I messaged Phil for the next few hours as I waited for what felt like the inevitable call to arms at 6.30am.

CHAPTER 10
I GET BY WITH A LITTLE HELP FROM MY FRIENDS

Just before we left John's the next day, Ken helped me bandage my arms. He explained the whole day was on my terms and if I needed to stop, we would. We would go as fast as I could manage, and any progress made was better than none. It was testament to the relationship we had formed so far that he had not shown any signs of frustration with me for getting myself into this situation.

We pulled up at our put in point and Ken and John unloaded all our gear. I was told not to lift too much but, in my mind, if I was going to paddle, I should be able to carry my gear, so I did.

Before long we were back on the water, I was still worried about if, and how, I would paddle. Was it going to hurt, would I be able to go at my normal speed or was this going to put a stop to my whole adventure? I soon got my answer, yes, I would be able to paddle but not without excruciating pain. Every time I lifted my arms slightly to move my paddles I wanted to scream out, I tried to hold back tears and just keep going, but after about 100 metres I had to pull ashore to rest and re bandage my arms, I felt that if they were tighter I they wouldn't feel to rub against the blisters as much.

Back on the water I felt slightly more comfortable, but each paddle stroke was incredible effort and we only covered 10 miles before breaking for some lunch. We then continued our journey 7 miles downstream to 'Antony's Landing' campground and called it a day. Ken secured us a camping spot next to a toilet, the site was once again for RV's only, so it was kind of the owners to let us even stay there. Once the tents were up I removed my top, cleaned up where the blisters had been seeping, reapplied my cream and lay in the cool breeze trying the best I could to relax.

It seemed our tents had caused somewhat of a commotion as within around 15 minutes we were surrounded by a group of young children asking what we were doing. They could not believe that we were staying in these tents that 'were so small'. Slowly but surely more and more people came to say hello, it seemed news had spread of our arrival and what we were doing.

Soon a lady who seemed to know all the children came over to introduce herself, it turned out she was the wife of the campsite owner as she invited us over to their RV for some pork loin. Before we knew it, we had a number of invitations all to different RV's on the site with everyone offering us food. We happily packed away our dehydrated meals and headed in the direction of one owned by a lady called Tammy who was adamant that we should come and say hello and share in her family BBQ.

Before we left our tent, a young couple approached us and handed over some muscle rub cream. They had seen us pull up at the boat landing massaging our aching limbs so had popped out the shop to get us something to help.

We sat outside Tammy's RV with her family and were treated like some form of celebrities, each person taking it in turns to introduce themselves and shake our hands. All manner of questions were thrown at us, some about the challenge, others about Great Britain and the one that seemed to be ever popular when an American realised we were British. Did we know the Queen?

Soon the children who had been talking to us earlier returned asking about our Kayaks and wanted to know how we could possibly live out of them, with them being so small. Ken took them all for a tour of the boats as I made conversation with our new-found friends. He had only been gone a matter of minutes when the lady next to me informed me of a vicious storm forecast for that night, she offered us the floor of the garage in her apartment saying we could put our tents up in there to keep us safe. I thanked her and went to tell Ken of the generous offer after all we had decided to make all decisions together.

As I found Ken still surrounded by the children we were once again approached by the young couple who had given us the cream, they introduced themselves as Greg and Diane, they too were concerned about the predicted storm that night and had come over to offer us their spare lodge to stay in. Another night in a bed, to what did we owe this kindness? We didn't need asking twice as we began to collapse our tents, Greg informed us that he would bring a golf buggy down to collect us and our stuff then take us to the lodge. It was only about 50 metres (a small walk away) but we thanked him and gathered our things.

We said our thanks and goodbyes to Tammy and her family only to be told breakfast would be ready for us in the morning at whatever time we needed it. We tried to dissuade them as we knew we had to be up early to make the most of the day, but we feared this would fall on deaf ears.

Deaf ears indeed. We were up at the break of dawn and began driving our gear to the boats in the golf buggy left for us by Greg to see Tammy up cooking us a breakfast of bacon and pancakes. She waved us over and we ate like kings. Given the choice we would have happily stayed there chatting away with all those on the campsite for the rest of the day, but we needed to get moving so we said our goodbyes and bid Tammy the biggest of thankyou's and headed back the boats. That was a night I would never forget, such kindness and hospitality shown by people who were at first, strangers.

On pulling out of Antony's Landing we were greeted with an incredible view; the sun was still rising straight ahead of us turning the clouds red and orange. The reflection on the water shimmered and it almost looked inviting, that was until the storm clouds came in.

I had decided to do away with the bandages on my arms, they felt more of a hindrance then a help, and instead that morning I rolled up the sleeves of my t shirt whilst the sun was low in the sky to allow the blisters to dry off. The rain helped to cool the charred skin and I felt refreshed for the first time in days. As soon as the sun was up and at its most dangerous, I had to cover up my shoulders the best I could.

Well today has been one of those days that will be forgettable – pretty uneventful but hard going physically. **Monday 1st September, 2014. Massy Marina**

The day passed slowly and although we made more progress than the previous day it was hard work. It was labour day (the last day of the summer holidays) and it seemed every man and his dog was on the Mississippi on either jet skis or in pleasure craft making the most of the day. This meant we had to negotiate huge wakes every time one of them sped past.

We stopped for a quick lunch break at a bar, I turned my phone on to see a number of texts one from my boss Shan asking if I would be able to Skype the divers at work that day to say hello. My spirits were lifted, it would be amazing to talk to everyone, I headed outside and sat on the dock. I quickly tried to log onto Skype, but my phone was having none of it. I felt gutted and when I received an audio recording from them all via WhatsApp. I broke down, hearing friendly voices shouting words of encouragement and being able to recognise each one just made me want to go home and back to normality. I sat for a moment to compose myself and replay the words of encouragement in my head. I could hear in all the divers voices their excitement and belief that I could achieve this, I wiped away my tears with a new sense of determination.

Once fed and watered we got back onto the river. I was still struggling to paddle properly, and my body ached all over. I wasn't holding the most natural position due to trying to minimise the pain in my arms and this was wearing me down. As the sun reached its highest point I was struggling, and felt incredibly dehydrated, not from a lack of water but because my body was using it so quickly to try and recover from the burns. I told Ken I couldn't go on much longer in this heat and we pulled up at the next possible spot to camp for the night. It just so happened to be a marina, with a bar, showers and Wi-Fi! Excellent choice.

After the formalities of setting up camp we showered and headed to the bar. Here the bar staff seemed very amused by us and our accents. They instantly clocked that we were British and once they knew what we were doing asked for a picture for their wall of fame. They asked us the standard questions of do you know the Queen? is Halifax a suburb of London? how did you get here? and the most bizarre of them all was…

"Wow you're British, do you know Elton John?"

We both let out a laugh at the randomness of the question. We had to disappointment them with our answer but none the less we had a good night's entertainment. I suggested to Ken that due to me struggling particularly during the heat of the day that we set off an hour earlier in the morning and make the most of the cool morning breeze. It seemed he had been thinking the same thing and we aimed to be on the water and hour earlier than usual, by 6.30 am.

We kept to our target and were on the water nice and early the next morning, we kept to this time scale for the remainder of the trip. Our days were now beginning to follow a pattern, get on the river early, Kayak between 20/25 miles, transport through a lock and then repeat in the afternoon. Days passed slowly as we would be on the river for 10-12 hours, thunderstorms were a plenty and the waits at the locks were becoming longer and longer as we encountered more river traffic. Alongside this the accessibility of marked campsites was becoming less and less as such we were setting ourselves a target milage and then finding somewhere that looked nice to camp.

One evening we pulled up on a particularly picturesque sandbar named Island 259'. We have no idea what happened to 'Islands 258' or 260, but that was its name according to our map. Camping with sand underneath us sure beat rocks and twigs, and we had a great night sleep. I awoke to find I had accidently forgotten to put a bag of bagels into a drybag and move them away from my tent, something (most likely one of the chipmunks we had seen running around) had had a good feast on them and I had to rethink my breakfast.

I was soon over my breakfast concern when I saw the incredible sunrise we were being treated to. Mist was lying on the surface of the river and the sun was creating yellow rays between it, I stood for several minutes mystified by what I was seeing, it was so peaceful and serene.

As I packed my boat, I let my mind wander, it was September 3rd meaning that three years ago I would have been starting out on my first day of climbing Mount Kilimanjaro. It seemed so long ago, and I chuckled to myself as I thought of my current surroundings and how I get myself into these types of things.

Once on the water, paddling through the mist as the sun rose was an incredible sight, I let Ken paddle in front and managed to get a few shots of him silhouetted against all the incredible colours, it looked stunning.

Conversation was flowing, and our topic was the books and TV series of 'Game of Thrones'. Ken had brought along his Kindle and was reading the books as we went along. I however, had followed and previously watched the TV series and knew the stories and what happened to each character.

Each morning for a good half an hour we would discuss where he had got to and what we thought about it all. It was such an important part of our routine that it turned into a compulsory task for Ken to read at least one chapter a night, just so we had something to talk about the next morning.

A few hours into the day we hit another flood plain on the approach to next lock. This particular plain was huge, and we struggled to make out exactly where the lock was at the other side. The 'treacle' was back, and it took us almost 2 hours to cross. On reaching the lock we had a conversation with the guys operating it to ask whether there was somewhere close by to eat. Apparently, just a mile downstream from the lock, there was a restaurant called 'Candlelight'.

The pass through the lock took a long time, I felt my eyes closing, and ended up dozing off for a few minutes.

When I had eventually summited Kilimanjaro 3 years before this moment, after throwing up a number of times, and eventually having to be dragged to the top, I had simply sat on a rock and fallen asleep (and as such I have very little recollection of the summit itself). I could now add 'falling asleep in a Kayak in a lock on the Mississippi River' to my list of bizarre places to fall asleep. I was woken suddenly by Ken shouting to tell me I was slowly tipping my boat over!

After what was certainly more like 4 miles, rather than the 1 we had been told, we pulled up in the marina below the 'Candlelight' restaurant. As I sat in my boat, I looked up to see the dockside towering above me, it must have been at least 1 ½ metres tall and I couldn't so much as reach my hand to the top, getting out of my boat was going to be tricky. Standing up in my Kayak trying to balance best I could I resembled something of a whale throwing myself chest first onto the dock side. Rolling myself over I eventually stood up and we made our way towards the restaurant.

On arrival the 'Candlelight' restaurant it seemed quite an 'upper-class' establishment, so much so that Ken contemplated heading back to the boats and changing his top. Although I was covered in sweat and dirt, I couldn't have cared less, as I was hungry. I headed to the bathroom to at least clean some of the dirt from my hands and face. When I saw myself in the mirror, what a mess I looked and just to top it off, I had my top on inside out. Sometimes I can be so classy!

The food we ate was nothing short of exceptional, so much so that we treated ourselves to a pudding of chocolate cheesecake (our first of the trip) and it was heaven.

Powered by scrumptious pudding we set off for the last 20 miles of the day. It seemed that cheesecake was great fuel for paddling, I was on a roll and could have paddled all day. With my iPod on, I was singing at the top of my voice to 'Brave' by Sara Bareilles and was focused on the task ahead. At that point, nothing could have lowered my mood. When Ken suggested stopping for the night as he was physically 'done in', I could have carried on for another 10 miles but agreed, it was better to finish the day with some energy in reserve.

We pulled over onto a sandbank below a row of houses and Ken went up to the nearest of them to ask permission for us to crash on their sand. Eric, the owner of the house, soon came down to introduce himself properly and brought along his daughter Ashley. They were heading out on a short fishing trip but said they would be back soon. On their return they invited us in to use their shower (obviously we must have smelt) and cooked us Spaghetti Bolognese. It seemed we were mini celebrities as it wasn't long until all their neighbours were around to meet the two 'Brits ' who were kayaking down the river. It was another wonderful night of good company.

A thunderstorm led to an incredibly disrupted night's sleep, and next morning we had to sit in our tents until 9.30am to wait it out, not the best start to the day. Tired and with wet gear, we eventually set about our normal routine, packed our kit away and got back onto the river.

I spent the morning deep in my own thoughts, I had dreamt of home that night and it was making me feel somewhat home sick, I shuck off the thoughts and paddled on, trying to make up for lost time.

As we approached our first lock of the day, we were told there would be at least a 1 ½ hours to wait before we could get through. Brilliant, this was not turning out to be our day.

Waiting did nothing for our motivation as we pulled up onto a small deck and set to boiling water for lunch on our stove, we decided we may as well make use of the time. Food eaten, we got back into our boats and headed in the direction of the lock, we knew we still had a while to wait but wanted to be nearby in case things changed and we could get through earlier.

I pulled up against a fallen tree and tied myself off, so I wasn't constantly having to back paddle just to stay still. A wind was getting up and I was soon being bounced around by a 4-foot swell, I untied myself from the tree as I was being smashed into it with every wave.

Finally, we were called forward into the lock and began the now predictable formality of finding the ropes and holding on while we were lowered down. In the 20-minute period we were sat in there the wind was getting stronger and once the lock gates opened, we were confronted with high swells coming straight at us. Not only this, but a few metres in front of the gate was a barge waiting to come up stream, it was terrifying being so close to one and as we paddled past it we were thrown off balance by the water churning out from the back of the tug.

Waves were getting bigger, bouncing back and forth off the barge as it churned out water at the back and this, combined with water gushing down the dam to the left, led to horrendous paddling conditions. I was being knocked side to side and was losing control. For the first time on the whole journey, I didn't feel in control of myself and thought I would be tipped out any second. I shouted to Ken to say so and suggested we get to the shore and quick, he must have read my mind as he veered off to the right bank. We desperately looked for somewhere to pull ashore and seek safety.

A couple on the right bank were making repairs to their house. They looked out towards us and could clearly see we were struggling. They immediately shouted over the wind, asking if we wished to pull ashore. I didn't need asking twice and had pulled up at the ramp to their house before Ken even had the chance to ask them to repeat themselves.

Introducing themselves as Tom and Arleen, the couple welcomed us onto their lawn and said we were welcome to pitch our tents there for the night, a bathroom in the basement was ours to use as we wished, and they left us to it.

It was great to pitch the tents on such well-kept grass; the pegs went into the ground easily and we knew we would have a good night. About 10 minutes later Tom and Arleen returned asking if there was anything we wanted or needed, and they offered to drive us to Walmart.

We took them up on their offer and proceeded to their garage where we saw their extensive fleet of cars: an MGA, a Corvette; an Oldsmobile 88, a Cadillac Deville, a Jeep and an RV. They later told us the deciding factor in buying the house had been the size of the garage which could accommodate all the cars. What a beautiful house it was. With the tour of the cars finished, we jumped into the Cadillac and set off to Walmart in style.

What should have been a quick trip turned into a long one as I managed to get split up from Ken. Just like when you lose your Mum in the supermarket I walked up and down every aisle to try and find him but was unsuccessful. Suddenly I heard my name over the tannoy …

"Will Grace from England please come to the automobile department"

I now knew where Ken was but as for where the 'automobile department' was, I had no idea. I started to make my way to the far end of the shop to try and find this illusive 'automobile department'. Finally, I bumped into Ken at the checkouts where we laughed off the situation and headed back to the house where Arleen announced she would be cooking us a dinner of Spaghetti Bolognese. It turned out to be some of the best I had ever had.

It was another great night spent swapping stories, eating tasty food, and hearing all about Tom and Arleen's 53 years of marriage. Incredible. I could have quite happily spent days there with them and the thought of leaving in the morning did not fill me with one ounce of happiness.

At 5am the next morning I packed away my things ate a good breakfast that Arleen had got up specially to make and was back on the river ready but not so raring to go. We waved goodbye to Tom and Arleen as I promised to myself that I would go back one day.

The day was uneventful up until the last few miles where we got caught in the biggest thunder and lightning storm yet. It was so strong that we had to get off the water as quickly as possible and were forced to take cover under our tarpaulin on a nearby mud bank. We sat there shivering for around ½ an hour until the rain eased and then set about bailing out our boats that were now full of water. I put on my waterproof jacket in a bid to keep warm and we carried on paddling.

After such great hospitality the over last few nights, it hit us both hard to pull up at our next camping spot, a grassed bank access ramp to the river. It resembled more of a mud bath; ankle deep grime and sludge that swallowed our feet as soon as we stepped foot on shore.

We must have both looked like Bambi on ice trying to negotiate the slippery slope up onto the flat patch of ground. Branches and weeds scattered all over the floor did not make this an appealing spot to stay, but we had no option, and begrudgingly, set up our tents. I began to remove my soaking wet clothes. As I took off my jacket steam was coming off me, so I laid my clothes over the top of my tent and changed into my spare set.

Some friends and fellow Rotarians of Kens had been in touch that day and were going to meet us with a picnic which filled me with mixed emotions. It would be great to speak to new people but at the same time, I didn't know them and felt incredibly lonely. I sat mostly in silence during the picnic, listening to their stories of Rotary and the good times they had all shared. I have always enjoyed meeting new people but have never found it the easiest of tasks and can find it hard to think of what to talk about. Writing this now, it seems laughable. I can imagine most of you will be thinking: 'What! You were kayaking the Mississippi for goodness sake, what better thing would there be to talk about'. In all honesty, the last thing I wanted to do when resting for the evening was talk about the trials and tribulations we were currently going through daily, as it only made me think how long we had left to go.

The barges really are quite monstrous. They are huge and you cannot see the 'driver' until they pass you as the tug is at the back. This gives off the impression that they have a mind of their own and are hunting you down. Never mind Daleks or Aliens, in films they should just use killer barges.

Friday 5th September 2014. Lock No 16 (the mud bath)

We awoke early at 4 am the next day to complete a radio interview for back home and set about packing our kayaks. I looked up-river to see a barge approaching the lock just below us; great, that meant we would not be going anywhere for at least 2 hours. Minutes later I heard a whirring noise and turned to see another 15-container monstrosity heading our way, Ken quickly scrambled for the radio to try and get permission to 'lock through' between them.

"It will be at least a 4 hour wait now guys I'm afraid. It will be quicker if you just walk your boats around to the other side".

Ken and I exchanged exasperated looks. Our Kayaks each weighed around 90kg (198 pounds), we were stood ankle deep in mud, and the guy in the lock thought it would be quicker for us to pull our kayaks up the hill and around the lock! Begrudgingly (an understatement at best) we began pulling our boats, slipping and sliding in the mud at every step, and making little progress. A message soon came through on the radio, having seen us struggle the barges had taken pity on us and would let us go through the lock ahead of them. Finally, some luck… if you can call it that.

We knew we were closing in on St Louis, the mid-way point of our journey, and hoped to be there in just over a week. Each day we would paddle, paddle, and paddle, doing whatever we could to occupy ourselves, from designing our dream homes to discussing the British Education system (sounds great I know). The days felt incredibly long, our destination further away, and our motivation was shot. Every day would be a mental battle against ourselves, trying our hardest not to breakdown in tears or concentrate on reality. I was exhausted physically and mentally and was beginning to hallucinate, believing there were bugs walking all over me or I could hear voices, and speed boats, that would never appear. At night I often woke up adamant that there were spiders all over me.

The only element of excitement for the day, if you could call it that, was when we had to try and find somewhere to stop for the night. We always hoped for a beautiful sandbar where we could watch the sunset, but whatever happened, once we had done somewhere near the target mileage for that day, we would pull up at the first convenient spot. It wasn't worth the risk of carrying on and hoping to find somewhere better to stop as we could be going on for miles before that would happen.

One evening we pulled up at a small harbour next to a bar where there was a party going on to see if we could find somewhere to stay. A steady flow of people began to approach us asking what we were doing as Ken went inside to try and find the bar to find the owner and see if there was anywhere, we could pitch up.

Sitting with the boats I was soon approached by a local who introduced herself as Jessica, who'd had a bit too much to drink. She'd squatted down on the dock side in what appeared to be an incredibly uncomfortable position and was swaying side to side with a bottle in her hand. She asked all about me and why I was doing this (fantastic question really). She was amazed and decided I was so inspirational that she was going to stop everything and go off and have an adventure herself. (Jessica if you ever read this, I take no responsibilty or credit for any crazy adventure you have since been on…)

Once Ken returned Jessica (with her newfound love for adventure) decided she wanted to help me get out of my boat. Now I'm sure everyone has encountered a very helpful drunk person in their life and it's always nothing short of entertaining. I pulled up into some vegetation, so I was closer to dry ground therefore making it easier to get all my gear out of the kayak. Jessica stood up, walked determinedly into the vegetation, and tried to pull my boat up a bit further up, when she was struggling to stand up on solid ground it was no surprise she fell straight over and landed with her legs in the water.

Somehow everyone stayed relatively dry and we said "goodbye" to Jessica (who then headed off in a boat with a friend) and got all our gear together. Apparently, we could stay on the lawn opposite the bar; the landlord assured us the lady wouldn't mind. In fact, he would have someone contact her to tell her that 2 'Brits' would be staying on her lawn that night. The owner soon came to meet us, and it sounded like half the town rang her in the end to inform her that we would be staying on her lawn. She invited us up to her house as she wanted us to meet her Rottweiler, Buddy…

I have never been a huge dog lover so the idea of going to meet a giant Rottweiler was not filling me with happiness. She assured me that he would be on his lead, she just wanted us to meet him, so he wouldn't attack us or our tents in the middle of the night. Great!

Buddy was chained up by something that resembled more of an anchor line than a dog lead and I felt my heart start beating that bit faster. As we approached, Buddy was let of his lead and came bounding towards us, I braced myself ready to be attacked as he snarled and circled us, I stood fixed to the spot hoping someone would come and grab him soon. He must have decided we were okay as a few moments later he returned to his guard position and settled down. Phew

Thankfully the next morning I awoke physically unscathed, however I was mentally scarred.

Just as we had been trying to drift off to sleep someone at the party had started up the Karaoke machine and we were forced to listen to some classics being murdered by the locals. On top of this it seemed we had pitched ourselves near a train line and not just any train line but one that would carry grain and coal all over the country. I had seen a few of the trains from the bank of the river and they could often but upwards of 110 carriages long. To top it off as they approached the crossing in the town, they would sound their horn 3 times, then do one long continuous 'toot' until all the carriages had gone over the crossing, given the length of the trains this could go on for several minutes. I counted no less than 15 occurrences of this during the night, to say I had a disrupted night's sleep was an understatement.

CHAPTER 11
MEET ME HALFWAY

Away from the trains and Karaoke we were back on the river and gaining on St Louis, our halfway point.

Even though the river was now drastically wider than it has been at the headwaters this didn't mean an end to obstacles, in fact the next day as Ken and I were happily paddling along deep in conversation we suddenly came to an abrupt halt. It seemed we had managed to paddle ourselves up onto a submerged sandbar. There we were, probably 200 metres away from either bank stuck and unable to move forward, there was only one option and that was to get out and push our boats along. It must have been an incredible sight for any passer-by as it must have looked like we were floating on water.

After a bit of pushing and shoving we made it to the edge of the sandbar where we snapped a quick picture of me looking like I was stood up in my boat.

After these few minutes of hilarity, the day soon took a turn for the worse as a headwind arrived. Incredibly strong, it made paddling impossible. So, we pulled up at a posh looking yacht club on the right bank hoping they would take pity on us in this weather and allow us to pitch our tents on their grounds. Again, the hospitality of the American people did not let us down.

Excitement followed as we were told to paddle round and into the harbour where there was a boat lift we would be able to use that was meant for yachts. It was huge! Ken paddled himself over to the general area of where the lift was underwater, someone on shore pressed a button and before we knew it Ken was being picked up out of the water. If only they had one of the lifts at every site that we stopped at.

Lift excitement over, we were shown to a nice patch of grass where we could pitch our tents. We were then given free access to the clubs Wi-Fi and bathrooms, so we could shower and catch up on Challenge admin. It was also Phil's birthday, so I set up my laptop and logged onto Skype to have a good catch up with him. Meanwhile Ken was chatting to some locals who just so happened to be Rotarians like him. They bought each of us the biggest steak I had ever seen in my life and told us to 'just go and cook it on the grill outside and then join them inside'. We gladly accepted, and I headed outside to sort out my steak.

Our evening then followed the usual format of questioning and storytelling. By this point, we almost had a script as to the answers we gave and who would give it. We joked back and forward about the differences between Brits and Americans with one member of the group suggesting that because we were British, we must have to kayak on the left of the river. It was a fun evening and we headed back to our tents feeling upbeat.

This didn't last long as I woke around 4.30 am that night with stabbing pains in my stomach and a sudden urge to throw up. Again, it seemed that after a month of dehydrated meals my body couldn't quite hack something as nutritious and rich as a steak. After a mad rush to the loo, I thankfully managed to get back to sleep, only to be awoken by a crack of thunder hours later. As I listened to the rain hammering on my tent, I curled up in my sleeping bag…we were going nowhere soon!

Finally, the rain let up slightly, so we sought refuge inside the yacht club for breakfast where the maintenance man had opened the bar for us to use. We discussed our intentions for the day over food as the rain began to lash down once more.

My eyes were soon drawn to our tents which seemed to be moving around a lot in the wind, I was concerned that they may be about to be ripped out of the ground and blown away, so we went out to investigate. As I approached mine, I could see that the two pegs holding down the back end had been ripped out and the material was now folding in on itself.

Worried about all my gear I quickly forced the pegs back into the ground and scrambled around to find the zip so that I could get inside. My heart sank at the sight.

There in the middle of the floor was my iPod floating in a puddle of water, not only that, my sleeping bag and some of my clothes were soaked through. I was mostly concerned with the iPod; music had been one thing that had been keeping me even the slightest bit sane on our hard days and the thought of continuing without this filled me with dread.

With the rainstorm not letting up we pulled our tents out of the ground and with them still half assembled, rushed towards the yacht club where the maintenance man had just opened up the large storage room. Once inside I pulled out everything, now soddened, from inside the tent and surveyed the damage. Other than my iPod all other electrical items were safe, but I would now need to dry out most of my clothing and sleeping gear. Thankfully the club had a free clothes dryer in their changing area next door, so I headed in that direction with all my wet gear and after around an hour or so most of it was dry.

Having hung my tent up on the edge of some yachts and other bits in the storage area it too had dried off slightly, so I used my towel to remove the rest of the water and packed it away.

We were now hours behind our usual start time and the weather was not giving up, with 22 miles to paddle for the day we knew we needed to get going.

Over the past couple of days Ken had been in contact with a fellow Rotarian named Tom Drennan. Based in St. Louis he had offered to meet us at the riverbank and source a hotel for us to stay in for a few nights to avoid the worst of the forecast storm. We were due to meet Tom later that day, so we had no option but to get going. Wrapped up in our waterproofs we bid the Yacht club goodbye and paddled out into the storm. Thankfully. it seemed luck was on our side and the rain soon passed, although dark clouds hovered over us threatening another down pour at any point.

First on the agenda for the day was to pass through the biggest of all the locks on the river; a 40-foot drop that would take us nearly 30 minutes to get through. The lock was gigantic, so much so that there were no ropes long enough to throw down to us, instead we were told to just stay in contact with the side walls as we descended. We felt so tiny in this huge water filled hole as we were lowered further and further down. Finally, over 40 feet below ground level the claxon sounded, and the gates opened for us to move out.

In complete contrast next up was the smallest and what turned out to be our final lock on the river at only 1 foot. So small that we were told holding on was not necessary and if we wanted, we could simply paddle around while being lowered. So of course, we did.

Rain soon began to pour again as we edged that bit closer to the outskirts of St Louis. About an hour before we reached our rendezvous point, we officially hit our 1000 miles paddled marker. This felt like a real milestone and as though we were actually making progress towards our goal. Being 'high' on our achievements our final miles went quickly and we were in good spirits as we pulled up onto the boat ramp to await Tom's arrival. 1000 miles of the Mississippi River paddled, not bad for 2 'Brits' who didn't really know how to Kayak.

We had no idea what Tom looked like so anyone who came within the vicinity of the boat ramp was met with a hopeful look as we began to unload our gear from the Kayaks. A jeep pulled up a while later, a gentleman bounced out and introduced himself to us as Tom, he congratulated us on our achievements so far and soon set about securing our boats to the top of his jeep.

It was a short drive to a 'Days Inn' on the outskirts of St. Louis where we would stay for a night to avoid the worst of the storm and once settled in, we headed out for a meal with Tom and his wife Joy, then the last thing I did before sinking into my bed that night was update our Facebook post to celebrate our 1000 miles achievement.

Next morning over breakfast Ken and I discussed our plan going forward. He was really struggling physical and wanted to extend our stay by a couple of day to allow himself to recover, this would likely mean we would have to miss out some miles of the river to catch up for the days missed. While this was slightly gutting, I knew a break would certainly do my body good and after how supportive Ken had been when we had to stop for my burns, it was time for me to return the favour. Also, a couple of days of in a city would certainly be better than pushing on and perhaps having some forced days off in the middle of nowhere. We would take a few days off and move a few miles down the river to continue our journey afterwards.

In the knowledge that I now had some decent time on my hands I made the decision to give everything I had in my possession a much needed clean. I put up my tent in the hotel car park, dismantled it, unattached the inner from the outer, and gave it a good scrub with baby wipes. I washed all my clothes through (some multiple times) and things soon started to smell a bit fresher.

Over the next few days, we spent time exploring St. Louis and taking photos at the famous 'Gateway Arch' on the bank of the river, we stocked up on all our supplies and I even managed to purchase a new iPod for a price that was approximately £100 cheaper than in the UK! I love a good bargain.

Not far from the hotel there was a variety of fast-food chains and restaurants. We tried Taco Bell among many others and even treat ourselves to a rather expensive Italian, but it was soon time to head back to the river and our dehydrated meals as our break came to an end.

We headed to the aptly named 'Trail of Tears' Campsite around 150 river miles downstream from where we had taken out. It was gutting to be having to miss out so much of the river but there was no way we could have made up the miles in time for my flight home and the time off had been a necessity. I rationalised it in my head with over 1000 miles left to go we were going to be more than making up for it.

Tom joined us at the site for the night as he wished to wave us off in the morning. All was going smoothly until he realised, he had forgotten to bring his tent pegs. Not to be put off he soon managed to erect his tent with a variety of rocks holding it down and we bid each other farewell for the night.

PART 5:
ST LOUIS TO VIDALIA, LOUSIANNA

'The difference between the impossible and the possible lies in a person's determination'
Tommy Lasorda

CHAPTER 12
DON'T STOP ME NOW

We were up and, on the river, bright and early the next morning. As soon as we pushed off from the bank the flow was moving us down stream at quite a pace, a quick check of the GPS told us we were moving at 14 miles per hour when paddling. This was incredible, usually it would take us around 2 hours to coverage this type of milage, Tom stood waving to us on the bank and before we knew it, he was a tiny speck in the distance. This sudden change in flow was due to us having now passed all the locks and flood plains meaning the river was now free flowing all the way to the Gulf.

Finally, being free of all the locks left me with mixed emotions. As much as they had slowed down our days with all the waiting around, they had broken up the monotony of the day, and broken the number of miles we had to achieve into smaller chunks. Our days so far had followed a similar pattern, paddle around 20 miles (about 4½ hours paddling), go through a lock, and then paddle another 15 miles (about 3½ hours of paddling). Now the miles would all be in one chunk and seemed so much more of a mental obstacle. On the other hand, leaving the locks behind meant we were that bit closer to home so 'every cloud' and all that.

We sped down river to a place called Cape Girardeau where Tom had arranged to meet us with some sandwiches to have for lunch. We bid him one final thankyou and farewell as he told us he would hop on his bike and cycle to the middle of 'Bill Emerson Memorial Bridge' about a mile ahead of us to take a few pictures of us from above.

Safe to say we couldn't see Tom on the bridge, but we knew he had been there when he later sent a shot he took. So big was the river now that we were just tiny specs, it's amazing he even managed to pick us out really.

Our day passed quickly and after completing what felt like a huge 41 miles in the day, we started to look for a place to camp. Campsites were non-existent this far down river and it was now a case of choosing somewhere that looked okay to pitch our tents for the night.

We were in luck as we spied two sandbars close by, one down a channel to our left and another just ahead. Given the side channel would be a short cut through the large bend in the river we chose this one and pulled up on the bottom side of it.

It felt like a tropical paradise, a wide expanse of soft untouched sand with a small flow of river water splitting it into two halves. The hot sand burnt my feet slightly as I tugged my kayak up and out of the water. Once finished, I sat for a moment to catch my breath and just to take in my incredible surroundings.

Next job was to pitch my tent. Of course, this couldn't be the picture-perfect campsite as the wind picked up and made this job nigh on impossible. Each time I pegged down one end of my tent the other would pull up out of the ground and start blowing around. I decided to move further onto the sand bar in the hope of finding firmer sand. Miraculously, after a further 6 attempts my tent was eventually pitched.

Within half an hour of pitching our tents we realised the river water running through the sandbar had begun to rise and slowly engulf the sand; in fact, a small stream was curving around behind us as well. Concerned we would get washed out we decided we should head across the water to the other side of the sandbar as this looked slightly higher.

I reluctantly collapsed my tent and without packing it away threw it into my kayak. I even wondered whether it would be possible to simply drag the boats through the water but as we weren't sure of its depth, we chose to paddle across it instead. I got into my boat, put my legs on top of the deck (my tent was on the floor!), and paddled the now 5-metre and ever-widening channel of river water. Given my paddles didn't hit the floor on each stroke it had been a wise idea not to try and wade across.

I arrived on the other side before Ken and began to pitch my tent ...AGAIN! Ken soon crossed the gap and was on my side of the sandbar. He didn't think I had chosen high enough ground and recommended moving higher. Exasperated I pulled out all the tent pegs I had just finished securing into the ground, picked up my tent, marched up the sand bar, and threw the tent onto the ground. This was beyond ridiculous! All I wanted to do was crawl inside my tent and relax!

With my tent finally up and secure, after what felt like the 50th attempt, I began boiling the water for our meal. Ken pulled both boats further up onto the sand and attached them to our tents; he didn't trust the water and his reasoning was, if they were beginning to float away during the night the movement would probably wake us up. Although I did agree with him, I just had no energy left to do anything about it.

The sun began to fade, and we were treated to another beautiful sunset. The diver in me could not resist doing a handstand in front of this; cue some spectacular photos, more so of the scenery rather than the 'handstand'.

At St. Louis Ken had calculated that if we covered 40 miles a day, we would be able to reach the Gulf of Mexico on the 4th October (which was earlier than our original plan of the 8th). I was fine with this idea as long as we didn't arrive any earlier than the 4th. If we did, it would reduce the likelihood of Phil arriving in time for the finish (he was due in on the 2nd). I was also happy with the idea of 40 miles a day as I knew we could do that.

On the sandbar that evening Ken announced he'd made a mistake when he calculated the number of miles remaining. He'd made his calculation from Cairo, Illinois (the official halfway point on the river), 60 miles lower down the river than where we had actually put back in and a point which we wouldn't pass until the next day. This meant we had not accounted for these miles and therefore we were a full day behind.

I did some quick maths and pointed out this wasn't a major catastrophe as it just meant an extra 3-4 miles a day to hit our end date comfortably. Ken soon agreed but stated we should be trying to do 55 to 60 miles a day to account for the loss and try to finish earlier.

I made my feelings known about not wanting to finish earlier. Phil had paid so much money to fly out and be there for the moment I finished, and as my parents couldn't get the time off work Phil was to be the only person there. This was the biggest thing I had done in my life and I wanted to share both the finish and any celebrations with him. The possibility of finishing the trip before he arrived was not one that I was prepared to accept, and I said as much to Ken. I knew he wanted to finish as soon as possible but I was frustrated that he wouldn't take on board what I was saying. Pauline (his wife) was flying out within the next week and therefore he was guaranteed she would be at the finishing point for him. If we picked up the pace too much, I would have no one.

After a grand meal of…yes you guessed it…mashed potato, it was time to turn in for the night (it was around 19.00pm). It was getting dark earlier, so we needed to be up early and make the most of the light if we were to accomplish 50 miles paddling a day.

So, have you ever been hit by a fish? A live one? That voluntarily jumped out of the water, landed in your kayak and jumped back out? No? Well, I have, and it was a surreal experience.

Sunday 14th September 2014. Colombia

The next day started in a bit of a panic when I woke to the sound of Ken rather loudly flexing his vocabulary. I asked what was wrong, his answer…

"Quick, get out, the water has risen and is about 6 feet away from our tents!"

Apologies everyone, but I can't write down the first words that came into my mind. I needed no more information to spur me into action and frantically scramble all my gear together. I began stuffing everything as fast as I could into the dry bags. Thankfully I now had this down to a fine art.

This being said, since the second week of the trip I had been struggling with sore tendons in my fingers. Having my fingers in a constant grip action on the paddles for hours at a time had left me unable to move or bend them when I woke up each morning. This made packing difficult at the best of times, never mind when having to rush to avoid being flooded out.

Suggestion …next time you are packing anything, try doing this using just the palm of your hands and without bending your fingers. I'm sure you will then understand my difficulty.

Once I had finished, I threw myself and my gear out of my tent (just like James Bond diving out of the way of an oncoming train) to see that the water had indeed crept up on us and the land to the front, left and right of us had completely disappeared. This has been a close call.

Thankfully I soon realised the water was now coming up only slowly, so I took the time to rearrange some of my gear so I could pack it properly, although it was safe to say this was the quickest packing either of us had done so far. It was a good job Ken had attached both our boats to our tents the night before or we would have been stranded on land that was rapidly disappearing with no way off. The consequences of that didn't even bare thinking about.

As bizarre as it sounds, getting our boats off the now submerged sandbar and back onto the actual river was not easy. Yes, the water had risen, but it had simply covered the top of the sandbar and the water was sitting on it at around knee height. We had to wade a good few hundred metres before we could even get in the boats without them grounding. It was then a case of sitting in the kayaks and attempting to 'bum shuffle' off the sandbar until the water lifted us clear of the sand. We were unsure where the sandbar itself ended and didn't fancy starting our day with a dip in the river.

The rest of the day passed as per usual without excitement until…

I was minding my own business listening to some music and the next thing I knew I had been hit across the shoulder by a baseball bat.

Well, it had felt like a baseball bat, but in fact it turned out to be a foot-long Flying Asian Carp which I must have startled. It had jumped out of the water, hit me across the shoulder, jumped into my kayak, and back out again.

My first thoughts; well, they certainly live up to their classification as an invasive species.

Unfortunately for everyone at home I was unable to capture the moment on video, not because my camera wasn't on but because at the time, I was filming a passing barge. It's a shame really because that video would probably have gone viral on YouTube, got us more publicity and ultimately more sponsorships.

That evening while watching the night draw in we started up a conversation with a couple of locals who just so happened to be Rotarians, they wanted to help us out and offered to take us shopping for supplies the next morning, so we agreed a time and place about 12 miles downstream in the town of Hickman.

Before our rendezvous we paddled through what felt like the 'Pride Lands' from the 'Lion King'...... miles upon miles of flat water and fog, lined by steep banks, riddled with trees, floating branches, and huge tree trunks poking out of the water. If you took away the water, you could have thought we were in a desert. It was deserted apart from the two of us and felt very creepy. I really wouldn't have been surprised to see the 'White Walkers' from 'Game of Thrones' appear out of the fog at any moment.

Hickman, while on the riverbank was not an easy place to get to. It turned out that the boat ramp was 1 ½ miles up a back channel and against the flow of the river. By the time we pulled our boats out of the water we were shattered. What had originally been planned as a short stop for supplies turned out to be a 'sit down' meal at a café; I wasn't going to complain, any length of time off the river was a bonus. A full meal and pudding were consumed even though it was only 10 in the morning. During the conversation we discovered that not only were the 2 locals involved with Rotary, but they had links with district 1040 which is where the Halifax Rotary Club (Ken's club) is based. What a small world it is!

Powered by our pudding, we were on our way again and I passed my time on river doing maths!

You know it's a boring day when someone like me who has always been rubbish at, and dislikes maths, voluntarily indulges to help pass the time. I had already worked out that we needed to do an average of 47 miles a day to make it to the gulf on the 4th October (only 19 days away) and I was interested to work out how many paddle strokes that would take me.

So, using our GPS to track 1 river mile, I counted out how many paddle strokes it took me to cover it; it turned out to be 760. Times this by the 47 miles needed per day would mean I would be doing approximately 35,720 paddle strokes each day. This, times by the days left (19) meant I had approximately 678,680 paddle strokes to do before I would get to the Gulf of Mexico. Yes, only 678,680 paddle strokes (it doesn't sound as many if you say the number fast!) Hurray! As I stuck my paddle into the river, I kept thinking that's one stroke closer and one less to do.

We were now well and truly in the South, having passed through Kentucky and into Tennessee. The accents had changed and so had the river. It was much wider than it had been in Minnesota, and at times was over 1 mile wide. While it didn't happen often, somehow Ken and I ended up on the complete opposite sides of the river late one afternoon. Perhaps it was due to my focus on arithmetic.

Our stop for the night was at New Madrid which I could see ahead of me on a huge bend in the river, on the right bank. My own plan was to stick to left bank and simply paddle straight across the river once it began to bend away to the left thus saving me both the time and physical effort off hugging the right bank and navigating the huge bend.

Ken however, unbeknown to me had decided to stick to the right bank and follow it round. We were finally reunited at the base of the boat ramp. Ken wasn't happy with me and he told me not to stray away from him again. Apparently, he had been worried for my safety when he couldn't see me. I explained my actions by telling him that I had been trying to conserve my energy by taking a shorter and quicker route.

We set up camp on what would be rated as one of our better pitches. It was beautifully flat with a healthy patch of grass and was surrounded by plants. It's only downfall ...it overlooked the river. When Ken left camp to go and buy us some food at the local petrol station, I managed to make an 'out of the blue' surprise phone call to Phil. The mosquitoes and midges were rife, so when Ken returned with food, we ate up quickly and then retreated to our tents.

If I campsite had been a delight, the next day was nothing short of frustrating. We spent the entire morning zig- zagging across the river to avoid submerged islands and wing dams. (Wing Dams are man-made features placed underwater to force the flow of the water into channels for the barges to travel down, however they create disturbances in the water such as whirlpools, and incredibly choppy waves).

It felt like we were making no progress at all and I was surprised and shocked when Ken said we had paddled 26 miles. At one point I was so frustrated with the situation that I threw my paddle into the water and decided to take a break for 5 minutes to calm myself down. I must explain here that I found it incredibly frustrating that I didn't have a map, or GPS (Ken had these) and being told every few minutes that I needed to go in a different direction just as I had picked up a bit of speed was incredibly annoying.

With warnings from 'Mr Monotone' (the weatherman) that the river would rise by over 9 feet during the night we decided to stop paddling for the day at the town of Caruthersville hoping to find a hotel to stay in. This was a few miles short of the 47 needed per day but it wasn't worth the risk of another flooded sandbar. We found refuge at a 'Holiday Inn' and spent the evening eating followed by a visit to the local Casino based on an old steamboat. I can assure you that we didn't do any gambling, but it was great to just look around.

Next morning, I woke up to find my legs were covered in bites. There must have been more bugs in the bed of the hotel than on the river, which I hadn't thought was possible.

They say you should do one thing a day to get your heart racing, well today we did such a thing many times. **Wednesday 17ᵗʰ September 2014. Boat Landing**

Before we had even stepped foot in America people had been discussing and often placing bets on how often they thought we would capsize on river. Ken had made the bold statement that we could complete the whole journey on the river without capsizing; I was more sceptical.

That being said, we were now more than halfway through our journey and I hadn't yet taken a dip in the mighty Mississippi, however the obstacles now being thrown in our path were bringing me closer and closer to the possibility of this happening. Two particular obstacles causing me havoc were the aforementioned Wing Dams and Dykes (also known as weirs in the UK- a big or small dip caused by an obstacle, often man made, spanning the width of the river). Over the next few days, we seemed to spend most of our time trying to avoid them. However, one morning we went in the wrong direction and straight into the path of two of the biggest we had come across so far.

We headed off down a marked channel that would cut out a huge bend of the river and therefore save us lots of time. Ken re-read the map and saw warnings of potential disturbances to the water; however, it was too late to turn back so we responded positively by pulling on our splash skirts and continuing to paddle while keeping our eyes peeled for potential hazards. A few minutes had passed when I looked ahead…the river was disappearing downwards incredibly fast!

My heart suddenly began to beat faster. We slowed down our paddle stroke and determined that we were fast approaching the so called 'disturbances'.

I shouted to Ken and suggested we tackle whatever was ahead of us, one at a time. If the worst should happen and one of us capsized at least that way the other person may be able to help out.

Ken went ahead I stayed back, paddling against the pull of the water. It wasn't until I saw the back of Ken's boat come up out of the water that I realised just how big a drop it was going to be. Ken shouted all clear, so I gritted my teeth and paddle forward.

It wasn't long before the water soon began to pull me forwards and down the drop I went. I can only liken the experience to being at the top of a 'Log Flume' ride, where you almost hover for a second before plummeting quickly downwards at a pace and get drenched in the process. Thankfully I managed to stay relatively dry this time, but my heart certainly skipped a few beats.

In the heat we pulled off our splash skirts and had a quick drink whilst swapping stories of the experience. Ken suddenly stopped.

"Wait what's that?"

"Erm it sounds like a train to me" I replied

"Oh **** it's another one, look"

I looked only a few metres ahead and suddenly felt my boat pick up pace. I was being pulled at speed straight into the next dyke. Responding quickly, I threw my bottle into my boat, re fitted my splash skirt, picked up my paddle and started paddling backwards to give myself as much time as possible to assess the situation.

A quick glance to either side of me was enough to know there was no chance of us portaging around it. Mud and trees lined the banks and even if we had managed to paddle against the pull of the water and avoid going down the drop sideways, ascending the slope to safety would have been impossible. There was no other option, we were going down it!

We used the same system as previously and Ken went on ahead.

"STONES!!" I heard Ken shout as he tipped over the edge. I replied to let him know I had heard, not that there was much I could do. I lined up my kayak head on to the water and started forward.

As I tipped over the edge, I felt the bottom of my boat buckle, I was thrown to the right and then the left. Bordering on capsizing, with the right side of my boat out if the water I could see I was heading straight towards a huge sharp rock that was sticking up in front of me.

I quickly came up with the idea that if I hit it on the left-hand side of the kayak it may keep me upright. It was going to be a risky decision, but I didn't have much choice, so I braced for impact.

Bang! I was thrown against the rock which then, as I had hoped threw me to the right and I regained my balance. My plan had worked, and I was back in control of my kayak. I now paddled forwards and away from the churning water. WOW! That had been a close call but after the monotony of miles of flat water it had been great fun.

After the adrenaline filled morning a stop for lunch was in order. Pasta was on the menu and we chose a package that we had purchased some time ago in Grand Rapids, before setting off. It had been sat there long enough and we both felt it was now time to try it. It wasn't our best purchase, but I think if we had allowed the pasta to cook fully, we would have still been there waiting. So, crunchy pasta and watery sauce it was…YUM!?

Our afternoon was a bit less eventful as we completed our milage (a new personal best of 50 miles) and pulled up onto a boat ramp for the evening.

Left: A quick picture I snapped of Ken as we made our way down river

Right: As the river became wider we felt smaller and smaller

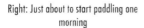

Left: My view for 58 days

Right: Just about to start paddling one morning

Left: Sheltering from one of the many thunderstorms we got caught in

Right: After another night on a sandbar packing my gear away for another days paddling.

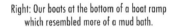

Left: We hit a sandbar in the middle of the river, so I got out of my Kayak for a quick walk. This shot makes it look like im stood up in my boat

Right: Our boats at the bottom of a boat ramp which resembled more of a mud bath.

Left: Being the typical tourist and posing for a picture with the St Louis Archway

Right: A particularly beautiful campsite, before we got flooded out.

Left: As the sun was setting on another day I took the opportunity to make the most of the moment and do a handstand in front of the sun

Right: On leaving Cairo, Illinois, Tom snapped a picture of us. The river was now huge and you can barely make us out. If you look really closely you can see two black dots in the middle of the shot.

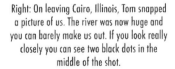

Left: Having a moment of contemplation after setting up camp for the night

Right: Taking in another incredible sunset one evening after celebrating paddling 2000 miles.

Left: Another peacefull campsite for the night, This was also the site where we were woken up by strange howling during the night.

Right: A particualy nutritious breakfast of Ramen Noodles

Left: With the Mississippi River Queen paddlesteamer in the harbour of Memphis

Right: Approching Baton Rouge, the largest industrial port on the River

Left: We managed to get some pictures of us next to one of the huge ocean going ships, thankfully this one was moored up.

Right: Getting back into our Kayaks ready for another day of paddling. I had mastered the art of balancing myself with my legs out of the boat by this point

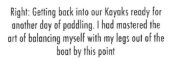

Left: Settig off for another day of paddling

Right: Mile marker 19, the sight of my emotional breakdown

Left: Finaly after 58 days we made it 'mile marker 0' and the end of the Mississippi River

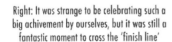

Right: It was strange to be celebrating such a big achivement by ourselves, but it was still a fantastic moment to cross the 'finish line'

Left: At 'mile marker 0' taking a moment to think about what we had just achived

Right: Once me and Ken had manged to get back to each other we got out our flag again and posed for some pictures

Left: I took a quick picture of 'mile marker 0' as we sailed away on the harbour police boat

Right: Finaly reunited after over 2 months'

CHAPTER 13
WALKING IN MEMPHIS

After paddling a huge 61.4 miles the next day we arrived in Memphis, Tennessee and on approach we passed the fantastically name town of 'Tomato'.

I felt surprisingly fresh to say we had just set a new personal best for miles completed but we called it a day and secured our boats in the marina.

We got a taxi to a local Holiday Inn and after trying 3 different rooms, (1 was filthy and obviously hadn't been cleaned, and doors wouldn't open for the 2 other rooms) we decided to head out to explore the city and to try to find the world renowned 'Beale Street'.

On leaving the hotel we approached a young couple to ask directions. Our mouths dropped open when the man spoke for there was no mistaking his accent ...it was that of a Yorkshire man! A quick chat told us he was from Hull in East Yorkshire. Imagine us finding someone from Hull outside a Holiday Inn in Memphis.

With the helpful directions we located Beale Street and passed the evening at a bar that had live entertainment. The female singer had an incredible voice, and we could have sat there for hours. It was a great night. We discussed our adventure so far, the highs and lows, and whether it had been what we had expected. Ken explained how he had been expecting to come across more river traffic, particularly barges, from the stories we had been told we had expected to see or come across barges every 10 minutes however, no such thing had occurred, and it was something if we saw 3 a day. Unfortunately, our time at the bar had to come to an end and we walked back to our hotel.

On the way I suddenly began to feel ill, 'rich food syndrome' was back with a vengeance and I couldn't get to the hotel quick enough. I felt so sick and uncomfortable, but I couldn't do anything about it apart from speeding up in the hope of getting to my room quicker.

In the morning we went down to reception to order a cab back to the marina where we had left our boats. We were told there would be a long wait, but the receptionist took pity on us and kindly arranged for a member of the night security team (who was just finishing his shift) to take us. This was brilliant news, or so we thought. It turned out that this particular member of staff had no idea where the marina was nor had any real geographical knowledge of the city, so we had to rely on our own memories to guide him there.

This being said there was a moment of entertainment via the radio. Back home it just so happened to be the day of the vote to determine the future of Scotland in terms of its independence from Britain. It seemed the Americans were extremely interested in this event, even more so than the people back home. It had been mentioned so often on American TV and everyone we had come across had asked for our opinions about it.

With us being 6 hours behind the UK the decision had already been made. The vote was for Scotland to remain part of the United Kingdom, the American radio station however seemed a bit confused and announced that Scotland had voted to stay a part of the British Empire…not quite the same thing but it gave us a laugh. It just goes to prove what is said in the media isn't always correct.

To add to my already sore shoulder and now stomach-ache from the night before, my wisdom teeth had been causing me pain over the past few days. I had been suffering with the wisdom teeth on both sides of my mouth on and off for approximately 2 years. As seems to always be the case my dentist had told me it would have to get infected several times before they would consider taking either of them out.

I'd had an emergency appointment with a dentist when I had been in Edinburgh at the Commonwealth Games because an abscess had developed for the second time. I was trying to keep on top of it as often as I could by smuggling salt out of restaurants, wrapped in serviettes, which I then used to help to keep it clean. Nevertheless, without a constant supply of salt, brushing and using mouthwash was having little effect.

We were now close to meeting up with Ken's friends in Lake Providence, Louisiana so he rang them to see if they could arrange a dentist appointment for me. I think it will be the only phone call he makes from a kayak on the Mississippi River whilst sat next to the world-famous, original paddle steamer, the 'Mississippi River Queen'. To our delight it had docked up in Memphis overnight. It was huge, and quite a remarkable sight. A boat so much a part of people's vision of the Mississippi River made us take our time to get a few pictures alongside it before heading out of the marina.

I still felt ill after having eaten the rich food from the previous night and was struggling to get comfortable in my kayak. I took some 'calms' tablets to try to settle my stomach and stop the cramps, but they didn't do much to help.

We journeyed on. Of course, following our comments the previous evening about the lack of barges we were soon met with an onslaught of them. Ken was now banned from talking about barges.

The only thing that could be said for the rest of that day was it was hot! We stopped at a huge Casino shaped like a castle to seek some rest from the sun and we found there was an 'all you can eat' buffet inside…challenge accepted! Having said that, I didn't know how much I would be able to stomach and, in the end, feeling like I did I was unable to take full advantage of the buffet.

The intense heat continued throughout the week. It was stifling, so much so that on one day we started to run out of water. We had to pull up at a house to ask if we could use their outdoor tap to refill our numerous bottles as we were going through them so quickly. Thankfully the owner allowed us to … the panic was now over. Running out of water would have meant the trip coming to a catastrophic end.

Two weeks and we will be finishing!

Saturday 20th September 2014. Sandbar

I will never know whether it was the heat affecting us or not, but one particular night spent on a sandbar could be called nothing but spooky. We pulled ashore and as Ken was seeing to the boats, I heard someone in the bushes going 'psssstt'. I turned to look but could see no one so I shook it off believing I was imagining things. Later that night I was woken by loud howling from what sounded like a wolf. I heard Ken let out an exclamation as we simultaneously went "what the…!" I won't lie, the noise unnerved me slightly. I started to think through what I would do if my tent came under attack. I soon realised any form of protection I had such as my paddles and knife were in my kayak (good one Grace). This fear was later heightened when I heard panting and grunting close to my tent. I told Ken who said it couldn't be true. I will never know if he was just in denial or whether he thought I had gone mad. All the same, I was adamant I had heard panting and of course naturally thought I would be eaten alive. Tiredness must have then taken over and I eventually got to sleep.

As I emerged from my tent the next morning, I discovered paw prints in front of my door that led off into the trees. I hadn't been imagining things after all! Ken then explained he'd thought he had heard voices near our kayaks in the middle of the night and had actually gone to look. This had been one creepy campsite and one we were both eager to leave.

Just before leaving we spotted freshly formed tyre tracks leading off into the bushes …how could a vehicle have been here…we were on an island? Thoroughly spooked, we quickly hopped into our boats and paddled away without looking back.

Our spirits were uplifted in the knowledge that we would soon be in Louisiana, our 10th and final state, and therefore closer to meeting up with Ken's friends. The days moved slowly but the miles were dropping. Each day followed the same pattern, up bright and early, paddle 25 to 30 miles, stop for lunch. and then paddle another 25. So much was it all just a routine that the days all began blending into one, although each morning to try and break up the journey and to prove to myself that we were making progress I attempted to go through the list of camp sites/hotels/houses we had stayed at, in order, in my head.

I also had playlists on my iPod that I knew would last a 25-mile paddle. The first thing I would do after our lunch break was put on a playlist knowing that it would be near finishing when we were ready to stop paddling for the day. I also became the fountain of all knowledge on how long albums lasted and how many miles we could paddle before each ended.

If you cast your mind back to the beginning of this book you may remember that I mentioned how I had auditioned for a part in a show. The show was the musical 'Whistle Down the Wind'. I had the soundtrack on my iPod and had discovered the first half lasted 59 minutes and therefore covered approximately 7/8 miles of paddling dependent on flow, the second lasted 50 minutes and therefore covered approximately 6/7 miles. It's no wonder I knew my own part and the words of every other character in the show by the time I got home. I had the time to listen to it more than 5 times a day. So, for those of you wondering how I kept myself entertained there you have it, making lists, doing maths, listening to music and learning my part for a show.

The scenery we passed never changed and the water…well it was still brown. Often our only source of entertainment came at a lunch break. On one particular occasion as we tried to burn the packaging from our food (as we always did) the wind was causing us problems. Ken decided to tuck the rubbish away in a nearby tree trunk to shield it from the wind, however it seemed the constant heat had dried out the trunk and very quickly the whole thing was on fire. Ken was peeing against the trunk to try and stop the flame as I rolled around on the floor laughing. We scrambled around scooping up water from the river and throwing it on the tree to stop the poor thing being burnt to cinders. We did the best we could and scarpered.

Following the burning tree fiasco, the rest of the day passed without much happening, that was until my eyes were drawn to a boat ramp where I thought someone was waving. I mentioned this to Ken, but he said to ignore it and carry-on paddling as our camp was only 3 miles downstream. I turned to carry on paddling but then noticed the figure had started waving a flag.

"Ken, they are defiantly trying to get our attention."

"We don't have time to stop camp is down there" he replied.

"They want us to go over to them. I'm going over."

I paddled across the current the best I could and pulled up on the boat ramp, as the man with the flag called out "Hello Grace". Ken had followed me across and pulled up while I was becoming acquainted with the mystery man, who I now knew to be called Park Neff (a local and River Angel), who had been waiting for us to pass through, hoping he could join in for a spot of paddling. Unfortunately, due to barge traffic, he had been unable to join us earlier on in the day so had instead brought us a selection of cold drinks and we chatted to him for a good half an hour before heading to our camp for the night, high up on a sand bar.

In the morning, for once, I was ready and raring to go safe in the knowledge that we would be arriving in Lake Providence that day where two of Ken's close friends, Triesch Trieschmann and Doug Seegers would meet us and host us for the evening.

Our plan of action for the rendezvous was that we would contact them once we had stopped for lunch and they would then set off in their boat and meet us somewhere on the river, wherever our paths crossed, I think that's what you call a solid plan.

Once back on the river we celebrated finally reaching Louisiana and stopped for some lunch in our 10th and final state. Less than 10 minutes after leaving our spot for lunch we saw a boat speeding towards us. It looked full and I could just about make out 6 people on board.

As they pulled up close to us, I spotted Doug (having met him once before in England). I felt a sudden sense of relief; this meeting had been arranged since day one of organising this challenge, but it had always seemed a long way off. It brought home to me that we were finally nearing journey's end.

Next thing to do was figure out just how to connect both us and our Kayaks to the boat so we could be taken up a side channel into Lake Providence itself. With them travelling at 30 mph however much fun it would have been to be towed behind them it wouldn't have been sensible, so we needed to get our boats up onto theirs.

A suggestion was for us to jump out of our kayaks and swim to their boat. We would then drag the Kayaks on board. However, I hadn't been submerged in the water yet and I wasn't going to if I could avoid it, after all I didn't trust the wildlife that may be underneath me. So instead, I stood up in my boat (quite a feat of its own) and holding onto my safety line I leaped onto the back of their boat. Using the line, I then dragged my kayak into the side and four of us lifted it up and placed it down the centre of the boat. Ken followed suit and his was soon on top.

Off we went speeding down the river at 30mph. We had left our GPS tracker on for pure entertainment, as we thought about those at home who would be wondering about the sudden increase in our speed and how were we managing to achieve it.

On arrival at the Trieschmann's, I had a quick shower and was then quickly on my way with Sandy, Triesch's wife, to see a dentist in the next town. It turned out they had managed to pull a few strings to get me an appointment. It was great to finally have the company of another female for the first time in weeks. We chatted most of the way there and back. The dentist was incredibly helpful and said although my teeth weren't yet infected, she would prescribe me with some antibiotics just in case they flared up again whilst I was still on the river.

On our return we cleaned our gear and the boats, I then attended to emails and other things that needed sorting out such as university assessments, and job applications. (Even in the middle of an adventure such as this the world has a way of catching up with you.) Once all this was completed, we headed out for a meal on the other side of the lake. I had my first taste of Alligator at the local restaurant, it just tasted like chicken really, but I would be more than happy if that was going to be my only run in with Alligators.

It was a lovely evening and it made me realise just how low I had let myself get mentally; the challenge was proving so hard. Physically I was just about coping, but my head was a mess, and I was dreading getting back on the river and away from friends.

They say all good things come to an end and before we knew it, it was time to get going again. Before leaving for the river the next day, Sandy presented us with a handful of military ration packs, also known as MRE's, along with a bag of equipment capable of keeping us safe should we be caught in a zombie apocalypse. These were from her own private store kept for such an occasion.

After cramming all the gear into our boats, we were soon back on our way. Trying out the MRE's was the highlight of our day as we both sat in awe of the technology. Watching our food heat up in a small plastic sleeve was nothing short of mesmerising and we thoroughly enjoyed the new tastes.

We managed to paddle a solid 50 miles before stopping for the night.

The next day after passing the town of 'Waterproof' (another original name) we received a phone call from Sandy. She had appointed herself as our tour operator and was trying to sort out safe stoppage points all the way to New Orleans (which we really appreciated). She had achieved success with her first attempt and that night we would be stopping in the town of Vidalia in the grounds of a church. All we had to do was ring a number on our approach and we would be met by the local vicar.

As we approached Vidalia I was on the phone, not to the vicar (Ken was doing that) but to my Dad. Yes, I was engaging in a phone call and paddling at the same time. With my phone balanced on my knee and on loudspeaker I was able to paddle, albeit a bit slower than usual. I continued to make progress whilst holding a telephone conversation and that for me was a 'win-win' situation. Ken and I managed to finish our respective phone calls, pulled up at the bottom of a boat landing and were greeted by the Vicar, known as Father Bill and his wife.

We secured our kayaks as much as we could, hiding them amongst some overgrown reeds on the riverbank. If they were stolen it wouldn't be the worst thing for Ken and me, we joked that by that point we would probably have searched for the thieves, not to try to get the boats back but to thank them for preventing us from carrying on.

Next stop was the church grounds. We pitched our tents on a perfectly mowed lawn. (Campsite rating 9 out of 10. It only lost a mark due to the hordes of fire ants that were eager to bite us.)

Father Bill wanted to take us out for food, so we drove across the river to the town of Natchez on the left bank, sat down in a busy restaurant, and had some great food. From our location, high on a hill all I could see was a winding brown line snaking off into the distance. Even from above the Mississippi still looked intimidating and I couldn't believe Ken and I had only been paddling down that particular section only a few hours earlier.

PART 6:
WESTMAR FARMS TO THE GULF OF MEXICO

'The man who can drive himself further once the effort gets painful is the man who will win' Roger Bannister

CHAPTER 14
BIG SHIP, LITTLE SHIP, NO CARDBOARD BOXES

Now starts the official count down. We have only 1 week left on the river, 7½ days of paddling, which is approximately 70 hours and about 302,100 paddle strokes left…yay…

Saturday 27th September 2014. Vidalia Church Grounds

I woke up the next day motivated and ready to go. Not only did we have only 1 week left, but that night we would be staying on a goat farm!

I don't think I have explained yet about my love for goats. If I go into detail it would be going majorly off tangent, so putting it simply … I have always liked them, would love to have one and they had become a constant source of jokes at work so much so that I did in fact have a plastic one strapped to the front of my kayak since day one!

West and Marguerite Constantine, another couple of close friends of Ken and his Wife Pauline lived on and ran a goat farm. They lived in the town of Moreauville, Louisiana that was around a 4.5-hour drive from the Gulf of Mexico and as such would be our hosts once we had finished our journey. We were now not too far from them on our journey down river and Ken had been in touch with them to let them know.

It turned out our planned stopping point for that night would see us camping close the Louisiana State Penitentiary so West and Marguerite advices us against this and offered to put us up for the night. Even better news what that Pauline had safely arrived with them a few days prior so we would be able to see her that evening.

We passed the boredom of the day by trying to come up with a title for my University dissertation. After all, once I was back at home, I would have to crack on with it, however much I wanted to pretend it didn't exist. We talked over all the things I found interesting within sports coaching and tried to think of some way of turning it into a research project. A few ideas came to mind. It seemed being in the middle of nowhere, in a kayak, is an effective way to 'brainstorm', although, however much we joked about it at the time, maybe researching boredom during expeditions and its effects on your mental health, would have been an appropriate subject for my dissertation.

At an unspectacular point in the day Ken announced we had finally paddled 2000 miles. It was time to celebrate and Ken encouraged a member of crew from a passing barge to sound their horn for us, which he did. As the barges left us to head North, we overheard them talking on our VHF radio.

"Did those guys just say they had paddled 2000 miles?"

"Yeh"

"I wouldn't even want to push the forward lever on this barge for that many miles never mind paddle it"

"I know. That's just madness"

We paddled away with a big grin on our faces for the first time in days.

It felt incredible to have made it to the 2000 miles point. So many times, I had doubted the moment would ever come.

As our day went on, I knew we would soon be reaching our stopping point for the day which filled me with excitement, and yet a strange sense of dread. I wasn't sure how I was going to deal with the emotion of seeing Pauline and the stark reality of Phil still not being in the country. While I was excited to see a friendly face, I knew it was going to be hard to watch her and Ken be reunited while I was still alone.

We turned a bend in the river, and I could make out two small figures at the boat ramp in the distance. I slowed down my pace to allow Ken a proper reunion with Pauline without him having to worry about me and how I might feel, I also wasn't sure if it would be too much for me to handle emotionally.

Unfortunately, my plan didn't quite pay off, Ken struggled to get out of his boat which meant I caught up as he ran over to hug and kiss her. I slowly pulled my boat up the ramp and got myself out as Pauline came towards me. Emotion overcame me, and I started to well up. I hadn't expected this.

She gave me a hug and tears started to fall. For the first time since we set off, I was finally seeing a familiar face and realised the end of the challenge was near.

That night we went to a restaurant where Michelle, West, and Marguerite's granddaughter worked. It was called 'Brown Bag Gourmet' and wow, the food was beautiful. There was a bottle of wine on the table with a label on saying congratulations, only 313 miles to go. We were finally nearing the end and it felt good.

What happened next was another of those strange occurrences. We were introduced to a 'fan' or a lady who Marguerite knew and had asked if she could meet us.

"'Wow, I'm a huge fan of you guys, I have watched all your videos and I really wanted to meet you. I'm so glad you have come here. Can I have a picture?" she said as she shook our hands and pulled us in for pictures. It seemed we were minor celebrities in the town.

What a surreal experience! She told me that I was hilarious, she loved us and our videos (at least someone was watching them) and that she was so excited to meet us. Ken and I later discussed how surreal this had felt. How strange it is that someone can make assumptions about your character from viewing a few videos online. It gave us a small insight into how it must feel to be a celebrity, where people judge you before they even meet you.

We were now closing in on the Gulf of Mexico and we knew it, but we didn't realise how much harder it was going to get.

As we paddled further South, I was becoming more and more aware of the impending threat of alligators and snakes (two of my biggest phobias) and with every log that I came across my heart skipped a beat, thinking I was about to be eaten alive.

However, the next day we discovered something much more pleasant on the water, a couple of fellow paddlers. This was the first time since leaving Lake Itasca that we had passed people paddling on the river. We called them over to the sand bar we were having a quick stop on. They were two friends who were moving to a new house. Instead of hiring a van to move their things, they had loaded up a canoe and were taking it all the way to

Baton Rouge…fair enough. They had a most fascinating story and were only a few days away from their finishing point. I almost felt envious. A few pictures later we were back on our way, pushing off from the sandbar as a group. It wasn't long until we had to pull away as unlike them, we had to maintain a certain pace per hour to reach the Gulf. We wished them well and said we would keep a look out for them tonight at our camp site where we could maybe share a fire or something but unfortunately, we never saw them again.

Waking up to a rainstorm was never a favourite pass-time of ours but we had usually been able to sit them out for a few hours allowing storms to pass before getting back on the river. That was no longer an option as we couldn't afford the loss of time. Our high milage requirements and lack of daylight meant we needed to be on the river early to cover the distances now required of us.

Therefore, that next morning we had no option but to pack everything away wet and just to add insult, hordes of ants had been climbing over our tents throughout the night meaning our tents were now drenched and covered in Ants. I tried to shake as many off as I could but as I was stuffing my tent in its bag, I could feel my hands being bitten

That day if all went to plan, we would be passing through Baton Rouge and I was excited to see it. It had been billed as both the most dangerous and impressive stretch of the journey so much so that many people had actually advised us to avoid it at all costs due to the busy docks and ocean-going ships. Clearly, we weren't going to do that, having sought advice from those who had paddled the river before us we felt prepared and ready to take on anything thrown our way. I was just looking forward to seeing it as 250,000 tonne ships were going to be quite a sight and I was excited.

We pulled up for lunch on a sandbar at a bend in the river just before Baton Rouge. Ken's reasoning was that perhaps we would get a view of the city from this sandbar and be able to enjoy it before concentrating on negotiating our way around the ships. Unfortunately, he was wrong, we couldn't see anything apart from each other and the dark muddy river.

Afterwards we discovered that if we had gone to the other side of the sandbar, just over the hill and around the bend, we would indeed have had a view of the city…typical!

Back on the river several empty docks slowly started to creep into view, it was almost eerie and very quiet. As we turned the next bend, there it was … Baton Rouge… huge, smoky, and silent!

Well, that was not what we had expected. So much for getting run over by a ship.

Somewhat underwhelmed I took a few photos of the big arching bridges over the river and the buildings on the banks, then put away my camera and took up my paddle.

After one stroke in the water my heart sank…

The flow had just completely disappeared.

How could this happen so quickly?

I was paddling frantically and making hardly any progress. Before I'd stopped to take pictures, we had comfortably been maintaining a 7 to 8 mph pace and now it felt like we were paddling not through treacle, but something much worse… it was more like tar. I would have made faster progress back in the UK paddling through the streets of London during rush hour.

This slow pace continued for the rest of the day. I was incredibly frustrated and let the rest of the river world (so no one) know. I was ranting to the sky and was angry at the whole situation. In all our research why had no one warned us of this? We had now set ourselves an impossible task! Making upwards of 50 miles a day in this flow was going to mean long hard days lasting longer than the daylight. I was furious and a few choice words would have been heard by others, had there been anyone there to hear them!

My shouting was soon cut short as I saw the bow of a large looking boat begin to emerge around the next bend, the rest of the ship soon followed, and I couldn't believe my eyes.

There it was our first sighting of one of 250,000 tonne ocean going cargo ships.

It was an incredible sight and I suddenly felt very small and helpless. Not only were these things enormous, it turned out they were also fast and silent. I felt like a little figurine floating on water in a game where a child was playing around with a submarine, making it fly past me. In the time it took me to digest what I had just seen the ship had sped by and gone.

Once we had recovered from the shock of seeing the ship, we turned our attention to our stopping point for the night, the town of Plaquemine. Once again Sandy had fulfilled her role as our travel agent and had located us a hotel to stay in for the night. All we had to do was find the lock at Plaquemine, go through it, and the hotel would be in front of us. This sounded easy enough…that is, if the lock still existed.

On and on we went trying to locate the lock. We saw the water tower with Plaquemine written on it, these were present at every town along the river, so we knew we must be close. Eventually we gave up on the lock and instead located a boat ramp ahead where we pulled up, hoping once we got to the top of it, we would be able to see the hotel. That didn't happen, but we did bump into a young woman who offered to drive us to our stop for the night. Once again, we emptied the kayaks of any valuables and tied them up in the reeds.

Once in the hotel reception we were told the lock was no longer in use and had been filled in. It was no wonder we couldn't find it! After a shower, I opened my soaking tent and laid it on the floor hoping at least to dry it partially before the next night. Unfortunately, it seemed I had also brought the colony of ants in with me from the previous night's camp. What a wonderful surprise!

Waking the next morning, I tried to stay positive, convincing myself that the lack of flow had been due to some freak weather condition or tide and that once we were back on the river everything would be okay again, I didn't want to contemplate that it could possibly be 'tar like' all the way to the Gulf of Mexico. My hopes were dashed as soon as a put my paddle into the water. The flow was still non-existent! It was going to be another long day.

That day the heat was stifling, and I could feel my face and arms burning. I pulled on a long sleeved top and wide brimmed hat hoping these may help me to stay cooler or at the very least stop me getting burnt…again. To top our situation off a few days earlier my camelbak water pack had broken so I was having to take breaks from paddling just to have a drink from my many bottles. Not an ideal situation in 3mph flow.

By late afternoon the day was dragging, and we were making little progress. Suddenly my right eye started stinging and watering. I tried to use water from a bottle to rinse it out, but no sooner had I done this than my left eye also started watering. This was great, both eyes were now stinging, I could no longer see where I was going, and I was in the middle of a river with barges and ocean-going ships steaming by. One of them could have been coming straight for me and I wouldn't have had a clue. I shouted to Ken who tried to help by pouring clean water into my eyes. Thankfully, after what felt like half an hour, my eyes miraculously cleared up and I could see again. I could only put this strange occurrence down to perhaps I had managed to get sun cream in my eyes.

With progress being so slow, we decided to stop at the next possible opportunity otherwise we would be paddling into the early hours of the morning to achieve the number of miles necessary for a single day. We also needed some extra time in the sun to allow our tents to dry out. We planned to stay in a house the next night and this meant we would be able to continue to paddle until later in the day and cover more miles, because we wouldn't need to set up camp. This would help us make up for the miles lost that particular day.

A Rotarian by the name of Carl had been in contact with us via our web page and offered to house us with members of his Rotary Club in New Orleans over the next few days. He was concerned about us pitching our tents either side of the city due to the high levels of crime and advised that he would meet us at a specific boat ramp the next day.

Meet him we did, but not before we endured one of the longest and hardest days of our adventure so far. It started brilliantly when a gentleman named Doug surprised us at our camping spot with a dozen donuts. He had been following our GPS tracker and noticing we'd stopped only a few miles upstream from where he lived, decided to bring us treats. I ate my 6 donuts very quickly and remarked to Ken how on any other occasion, eating 6 donuts within the space of a few minutes would be frowned upon. At that point I didn't care, they were good, I would burn them off within hours and they helped to cheer me up.

That day we passed several more ocean-going ships, and I began to note where they were from and just how big they were, Sweden and Africa were just some of the places marked on the bows. Most had 3 to 5 storage areas on board where they would store coal or grain. Each of these had a door that opened out in 2 halves from the middle. The doors were each large enough to have a helicopter landing pad marked out on it, so that was a potential five helicopter landing pads on one ship! WOW!

After 12 hours of paddling, we were approaching the outskirts of New Orleans and the last 2 miles of our day. 2 miles that turned out to be some of the most terrifying of our whole journey.

Barges were moored up all along the right bank of the river and numerous ships and barges were steaming past us constantly. Each time this happened the wakes would send us bouncing around as normal, but they would then bounce back off the moored barges and hit us from both sides simultaneously. I felt so out of control and scared for my safety. Ken was only a few meters ahead of me but often due to the high swells I couldn't actually see him. It felt like I was on a roller coaster dropping in and out of huge dips and being thrown all over the place. I tried to focus on keeping upright, terrified of what might happen if I capsized at that point, with so much traffic on the river I would have probably been sucked under an oncoming barge and that would have been it.

After all the effort of trying to stay upright my arms quickly began to tire, and I was struggling to keep going. My arms were aching so much, and I felt like I couldn't manage another paddle stroke.

I was thrown back to the moment on Kilimanjaro 3 years ago, where on my way to the summit I had collapsed from exhaustion onto a rock and 'puked my guts up', when after every 10 steps my legs had given way and I'd fallen to the floor, and when two guides had to grab my arms from either side just to keep me on my feet. At that moment on the mountain, and in that moment on the river all I wanted to do was give up and go home regardless of the fact that I was a matter of metres or days away from completing each challenge. I knew at that point that I was going to have to dig deep if I was going to get myself through the next few days.

Carl had advised us that once we had made it under the first bridge to keep an eye out for a boat ramp on the right-hand side of the river where he would meet us. However, we were now at least 2 miles downriver from the bridge and had yet to find said boat ramp.

I was near to tears, my arms hurt so much, and I just wanted to finish for the day. Giving up our search we pulled into a mud banking and got out. Ken phoned Carl and tried to arrange our meet up, it turned out we had somehow missed the boat ramp and were now standing in an area known as 'chemical alley'. Chemical, Ammonia and Steel plants lined the river at this point and all their waste toxins and poisons were in the mud that lined the banks, the same mud that we were now covered in.

Eager to get out of the toxic sludge we pulled our boats as high as possible from the water and waited for Carl to arrive.

With our boats strapped to the roof of his car we made our way into New Orleans. It felt like we did multiple laps of the city before we arrived at our hosts for the night. On arrival a young, cheerful looking lady introduced herself to us as Adele and warmly welcomed us into her home. Again, it seemed our arrival had been a cause for a friendly gathering and a number of Adele's friends came round for food. A delicious meal and a chat helped to cheer me up a bit, and I was looking forward to a night in a bed.

Adele and all her friends were also Rotarians and we would be seeing them again once we had completed our journey at a 'do' hosted by their clubs. Carl told us he had been in touch with the harbour police down in Venice (the last town and civilisation before the Gulf of Mexico) arranging for them to come and collect us from 'mile marker zero'.

A common misconception is that the Mississippi River ends at Venice or to some people even New Orleans itself, this is incorrect with 'mile marker zero' actually being 10 miles below Venice and 100 below New Orleans respectively. Therefore meaning, unless you have a boat to pick you up, paddlers have to paddle back up stream the 10 miles to Venice after reaching the Gulf. This wasn't something me and Ken wanted to be doing.

As we pulled away from the shoreline the next morning, waving goodbye to Carl, I looked forward to seeing him, Adele and all their friends again soon.

Back on the river our day passed quickly. Given our bigger milage days higher up the river we were able to lessen the miles needed slightly and our target was 25 for the day. This would also allow us to stay with more of Carl's friends South of the city.

We passed right through the centre of New Orleans, where Ken pointed out places I should visit once we had completed the river and when Phil and I would be spending a few days in the city. There was a momentous moment as we rounded the final bend out of the city and saw mile marker 100. We only had 100 miles to go. Easier to say then do though.

We met our host for the night, Heidi, at our designated spot; a mile marker signalling around 75 miles to go. With no way of properly securing our kayaks to her truck we lowered the tailgate pushed them into the vehicle as much as possible and secured them by simply sitting on top of them, not something you would ever get away with in the UK.

After freshening up we went out to a local restaurant for dinner with Heidi and her husband, we were talking about the challenge and all the highs and lows we had come across. We then got to talking about the remaining miles and this led to Ken and I's first argument of the whole trip.

Ken began to talk about the plan for the next morning and how we would be getting there, he asked Heidi if she would still be okay with the plan of dropping us off at mile marker 30. Given we had just pulled out at mile marker 75 I'm sure you can understand my confusion.

Conversation continued and it seemed the decision had been made; we would be cutting out more miles. I had not realised, been told or consulted as to whether this plan was okay. I was frustrated and angry. I had said all the way back up in St. Louis that I didn't want to miss out any more miles unless it was for an emergency reason, and as far as I could see, there was no emergency or threat to our life.

I already felt bad enough about the miles we had missed so far and, unless the circumstances were unavoidable, I wanted to complete all the river from that point. To then hear the decision had been made to cut out a further 45 miles frustrated me, and I said as much. To avoid making the evening awkward we said we would leave it and talk about it once we got to the house.

I wasn't happy and Ken knew it. I was angry that from day one he had said we would make all decisions together; at this particular moment this had not been the case and it was this fact that annoyed me most. We took the time to talk it through and he told me he couldn't physically do the 75 miles we had left, and that if we attempted it, he knew he would not make the finish. My anger abated, now I knew there was a good reason for his decision. After all we had been through together, I knew it wouldn't be right or fair to ask him to suffer more than we both had already, so I swallowed my pride and agreed to the decision. Ken apologised for having gone back on our agreement to make all decisions together and understood that my frustration had been with this and not the actual missing of miles.

We now had 2 days left on the river and 30 miles to go…or so we thought.

You could be forgiven for thinking that the penultimate day of the adventure would be glorious and happy. Well, it wasn't.

Our 57th day will forever go down as the worst of the whole trip, blowing all the other difficult days out of the water.

It didn't get off to a good start when Ken delivered some bad news. There had been a major error in communication, and we hadn't put in the river at mile marker 30 as planned, instead we were 20 miles higher upriver near mile marker 50.

This now meant a 40-mile paddling day instead of the 20 we had expected.

We were both exhausted physically and mentally and this news broke us both. We sat there deflated not paddling for a good 5 minutes. Doing double the milage we had planned to do that day felt like more like a request to go and climb Mount Everest in nothing but our shorts and T Shirts.

To add to insult it began to rain. We felt helpless.

There was a slight reprieve to the dullness of the day, when for the first time on the whole journey we had a tail wind. Paddling suddenly became easier and it felt more like we were surfing than paddling being pushed along my small waves. This didn't last for long though and we were soon back to the norm or headwind and rain.

To pick ourselves up we decided to have 'brunch' stop. We stopped paddling for 10 minutes and allowed ourselves to float along as Ken dug out the bagels and Nutella from the hatch at the back of my boat. We then proceeded to pass a knife, the bagels and Nutella from one boat to another as we had ourselves a feast. I think it was testament to our improved paddling skills that we were able to do this while floating along the river and not capsizing.

Break over, it was time to get back to reality and the large number of miles we needed to cover. It was a long. hard day but we were making slow progress, I took note of each mile marker as we passed…20…19…18…

Then at mile marker seventeen I hit my lowest point of the whole trip.

We were stuck in a crosswind that was causing my Kayak to constantly veer off to the left and my shoulder was throbbing with the pain of trying to keep myself in a straight line. We were trying to keep to the right bank of the river so as to stay out of the path of ships and barges but on every paddle stroke I was being pushed further and further to the left and into the rivers main channel.

To compensate I was paddling solely on the left-hand side trying to keep myself as straight as possible, the pure physical effort to do so against the wind was causing my shoulder to send shooting pains all down my arm and back, I was in agony and getting nowhere.

Being so close to the end but not being able to go in the direction I needed to be was so frustrating. Tears soon turned to anger as I threw my paddle down and screamed at the top of my voice. I was ranting to the sky. How could it all be so hard now with only 17 miles to go until we reached the Gulf of Mexico? Why would my kayak not go in a straight line? Why couldn't I just get out now? Screaming and shouting I let out all my feelings and stretched my vocabulary to the maximum. I just wanted to be off the river. I wasn't enjoying myself at all or by any stretch of my imagination. I no longer cared about getting to the Gulf of Mexico anymore. I had already paddled 2333 miles so what difference did another 17 make? I must have looked like a child having a big paddy as I smacked my kayak and screamed at it to go straight, but I didn't care, I'd had enough, I was mentally broken, and I was done…

CHAPTER 15
ONE DAY MORE

An hour later as I was contemplating paddling over to the shore and giving up for good the wind began to drop, and I was able to gain some control of my kayak once more. Again, I wiped away the tears, put my head down and continued the torture that was paddling. I told myself that if I could just get to the end of the day then maybe just maybe I could make it to the end.

It felt to take an age, but we finally reached the turn off for Venice and its marina as the sun began to set. I looked out to the horizon ahead. Somewhere down there was the Gulf of Mexico and if all went to plan, we would arrive there tomorrow…

Over a mile up the side channel, we still hadn't found the marina and hotel we would be staying in. Ken phoned through to get directions (yes, we needed them, the channel split into two) and no sooner had he put the phone down than a boat full of fisherman pulled up next to us. They offered us a lift to the marina as they were heading there. We happily pulled the kayaks on board.

On arrival we checked into a room and headed for some food. When we were eating, I got a message from Phil who was now in America, asking me to urgently ring West. I passed the message onto Ken and he rang through.

Ken went quiet. I could see from the expression on his face that something was wrong, but it wasn't until he had hung up that he told me what had been said. Apparently, the harbour police boat that was coming to collect us from mile marker zero, was not allowed civilians on board. This meant neither Pauline nor Phil would be able to come and see us finish our epic 'Mississippi Challenge'. I was devastated. From day one both Ken and I had imagined that Pauline and Phil would be there to share the moment we finished with us, but now we would be alone. I went to bed with not an ounce of happiness in me.

The boat that is coming to drag us back up from mile 0 does not allow public on board, therefore, neither Phil, Pauline or any of our friends can come and see us finish or get pictures of the big moment. I am gutted, this has just topped off my day. So, we will be ending like we began 2 kayaks the Mississippi and us, what an anti-climax. **Friday 3rd October 2014. Venice Marina**

I woke up in the morning and rang my parents. I had planned to ask Phil to Skype them as we finished so they could see the moment we crossed the 'line'. I was upset at having to tell them it wouldn't be possible because Phil wouldn't be there. All I had wanted was for them to see the end. They had supported me throughout this whole adventure and now they wouldn't get to see it finish. My Dad tried his best to cheer me up and had these words for me…

"I know it's disappointing but, in some ways, there is something quite poetic about it, you and Ken started it together and you will finish it together, just you two. You're so close now it will be over soon. I'm so proud of you."

As hard as it was to accept the situation, I knew that what my Dad had said did make sense. Ken and I had started this together, so there was certainly something about it just being us at the finish. I just had to accept the situation for what it was.

We decided to have a sleep in the next day as after all we only had 10 miles left to go and we wanted to give West, Marguerite, Michelle, Phil and Pauline the chance to complete their 5-hour drive down to Venice, so they could at least be at the marina when we finally arrived back.

At 10.30 am we packed away our equipment for the last time and pushed our boats into the water. This was it; we were finally going to finish!

It was nearly over. I felt neither happiness nor sadness, I just felt numb. I simply put my paddle in the water and began the pattern that had been my life for the last 58 days…paddle left…paddle right…paddle left…paddle right.

We were around 2 hours away from reaching the end of the Mississippi River.

Or so we thought.

Forty-five minutes later and we hadn't even made it back up the channel to the main river, in fact we hadn't even managed to paddle a mile. The wind was so strong it was pushing us backwards. Water was spraying up into my face as boats sped past with no regard for us.

We could see the harbour police's boat moored up ahead on the left bank, so we paddled over to introduce ourselves. They peered over the side to look at us and we introduced ourselves as the Brits they would be helping in a few hours. They pulled us on board saying they would take us out to the river, or we would never make it with the wind. Whilst we waited for the rest of the crew to come aboard, we got talking to those already there. One lady it turned out, was from Lancashire (the county in the UK next to Yorkshire). There's a well-known rivalry between the Yorkshire folk and the Lancastrians and this was cause for some good friendly banter.

Once the boat dropped us off back into the main channel we were faced with our best friend from the previous day, the cross wind; it made me angry, not now when I was so close, why for a single day out of the 58 days we had been going couldn't it just be an easy wind free paddle?

I was so frustrated that when Ken tried to calm me down by saying we only had 10 miles left I 'lashed out' at him and he replied in the same manner. Here we were on the final day, only 10 miles from the end, and we were shouting at each other.

Throughout the journey people had always tried to keep us motivated by saying things such as "you only have 100 miles left, that's nothing compared to what you have done". We greatly appreciated all the support but at the same time 'only 100 miles' was easy to say but when every paddle stroke hurt those 'only' miles were excruciatingly hard and seemed impossible. So, when Ken said this exact thing to me it set off a ticking time bomb.

I took a few minutes to calm down and apologised to Ken. After all I wasn't angry at him but was angry with the situation. We pulled our boats together and sat for a moment surveying the scene and thinking about what we were doing. In silence I pulled out my final packet of beef jerky and offered Ken some. He took it but soon spat it out saying it tasted disgusting. The fact it had been in my bag 2 months may have had something to do with it. Ken laughed as I threw the remainder of it in the river saying maybe the Alligators and Sharks might enjoy it. We gave a quick nod to each other and carried on.

5 miles down, 5 more to go…

6 miles down, 4 more to go…

7 miles down, 3 more to go...

"So, Ken, where exactly is the finish?"

For the next 15 minutes we had a debate as to where mile marker zero actually was. Believe it or not there is no signpost signalling the end point, no passport control, and no 'we hope you enjoyed your stay, come back soon' sign. All we had to go off were the maps and GPS. Ken knew the official end of the river was at the point we crossed the 29 degrees' latitude line, so for the last 3 miles he was counting down on his GPS while I was trying to follow the mile markers that seemed to have suddenly disappeared.

Minutes later I could see something sticking up at the head of what looked like a number of channels. Another 2 miles passed, and I now recognised it as a mile marker. That had to be mile marker zero. I was a mile away, 790 strokes away, about 15 minutes away. I suddenly started to speed up. It was here. Our Mississippi Challenge was finally going to end.

About ½ a mile away from the marker Ken started counting down, he shouted that we were close to crossing the 29 degrees' line. 3…2…1…he reached zero and raised his arms in the air.

"MADE IT" I heard him shout.

Everything happened so quickly, and I was paddling ahead of Ken as he shouted. It didn't feel right for me to just stop and say I had finished. I could see the mile marker that I knew would have a big zero on it ahead and suggested to Ken that we paddle there just to be sure we had finished. We didn't want to finish a matter of meters short when we had come all this way.

I fixed my gaze on the mile marker ahead and continued paddling. Each paddle stroke was bringing me closer to the end but the last ½ a mile went on forever.

400 metres left….

200 metres left….

100 metres left….

I was paddling as fast as I could as I looked ahead to the mile marker on my right, in front of me. I could just about make out the huge zero on top, and it was getting closer…

Faster, faster…2 metres away, come on, come on!

As I took my last stroke of approximately 1,786,000 I raised my arms in the air…. looked up to the heavens and simply screamed out…YES!

We had done it! It was over! We had paddled the length of the Mississippi River!

I sat in silence with my head in my hands. No more kayaking. No more pain. No more crosswind. That was it…, it was over.

CHAPTER 16
THE END WHERE I BEGIN

I sat there in silence. I didn't cry, I couldn't, I was drained of all emotion, it was just a sense of relief that brought a small smile to my face.

There wasn't much time to celebrate as before I knew it, I was very quickly being dragged down the channel by the wind and a sudden surge of what was now tidal water. I shouted over to Ken and we quickly paddled towards a set of stakes sticking up to the right of the channel. We held on for dear life, not wanting to get dragged out into the ocean. The harbour police boat was nowhere to be seen and I was being thrown into the wooden stake with every wave, all I could think of was' what a way to end this.'

Finally, a good 15 minutes later, the harbour police boat appeared, but getting to it was not going to be easy with the wind and waves. Thankfully a small boat with some fishermen in spotted me and came to my aid, they could see I was struggling against the current. In fact, I was in a situation where it was impossible to paddle against the tide. If I had let go of the stake I would have been swept out to sea incredibly fast and probably halfway to Cuba before I knew it. The fisherman came as close to me as they could, and I grabbed on to the edge of their boat. They managed to hold me there and took me to the harbour police boat.

Once alongside, the men on board grabbed hold of the side of my kayak and I jumped out for the final time. Ken soon joined me, and with a huge grin on his face we shared a hug. We lifted both boats up onto the deck a good metre above us, secured all our equipment, and Ken then headed inside. Alone on the deck I took a moment to try and let everything sink in. I took out my phone and snapped a quick picture of 'mile marker zero'. Heading inside I was surprised to see I had a signal so I rang my parents to share the news. It was a surreal moment hearing their voices and knowing it was all over.

The trip back to the marina felt to take an age and I was so excited to see Phil. It had been 2 months since I had left him at Manchester Airport. The Captain of the boat slowed down to the speed limit as we re-entered the side channel to Venice, when all I wanted was to go full speed back to dry land. We finally took a right turn back into the marina and I joined Ken out on deck where he had his union flag flying high. There they were, Phil and Pauline with West, Marguerite and Michelle sat on the dock side waiting for us. The Captain switched on the sirens to announce our arrival, I took one look at Ken and with the flag raised high above us we both burst into tears. It was really over.

As we were approaching the dockside, I had to resist all temptation to jump the gap and hug everyone. We finally pulled up, unloaded the kayaks and I leapt over the back of the boat and straight into Phil's wide-open arms. As I buried my head into his shoulders, I simply said

"Never let me do anything like this ever again...and I'm sorry if I stink"

PART 7:
EPILOGUE

'It always seems impossible until it's done' Nelson Mandela

CHAPTER 17
BACK TO LIFE, BACK TO REALITY

Phil and I spent the next couple of days in New Orleans staying with Bart, a Rotarian I had met at Adele's.

The first night we attended a bowling party hosted by the Rotary Club Carl was a part of. It was lovely to celebrate us completing the trip but all I really wanted was my bed and some down time. Ken came up to me during the evening and asked how I was. I simply told him I was overwhelmed being surrounded by so many people, he agreed. After 2 months of just each other for company, being in a room with 100 other people felt strange.

We spent the rest of our time in America at West and Marguerite's house, where we got to see the goats and just have some well-deserved down time. I washed all my kit multiple times, but it seemed my tee shirt would never come clean again. My tent finally smelt fresh again even if I did snap a pole when putting it away (at least I hadn't done that during the trip itself). We cleaned out the Kayaks as we were hoping to sell them on to help recoup some of the money for the trip and I wasn't sad to be seeing the back of them. It was great to be able to sleep in a bed again even if most nights I woke up in fear that it had all been a dream and that I hadn't even started yet.

Our final week flew by and before I knew it, we were on our way home. Sitting in a plane flying over the Mississippi was surreal I couldn't believe I had been down it. Finally, being reunited with my family was emotional, my Dad hugged me as I walked through the door, but my brother was on the loo and my Mum was busy upstairs, so I had to go and find them.

I was back to reality very quickly. It felt such a long time since I had last seen them, they surprised me by inviting all my Aunties, Uncles and Cousins over for bacon butties which was a nice touch. It was great to have proper bacon, no offence to any Americans but it's just not the same there. Miraculously I suffered no jet lag even though we had flown overnight, and I had slept very little, I just forced myself to stay awake all day.

A few days later I went into work, simply to visit everyone and received quite the welcome home being hounded by every diver in the room. It was great to see everyone again and life soon began to return to normal (whatever that is). I was soon back at University and trying to refocus on everything.

The first 6 months following my return were incredibly hard; I felt lost as though I had nothing left to focus on. Most of the past year had been focused on the Mississippi Challenge and now it was over it felt as though I had nothing to aim towards or look forward to in my life. My motivation to do University work was at rock bottom and life just plodded on slowly with little excitement. I couldn't even motivate myself to go through all the videos and pictures I had taken or begin writing this book.

It took time but things slowly began to return to normal. Requests for me to go to different functions and talk about my experience were flying in. With each one of these my reflections on the whole experience slowly began to change. The first one I did probably no doubt gave the impression that it was the worst thing I had ever done (at times that was true) but a few months later on this changed and I could reflect more positively on what I had learnt about myself, how I had changed as a person and what an adventure it had been.

CHAPTER 18
1 YEAR ON

So today marks a year since we finished our journey down the Mississippi. I have just finished work where the divers brought candles and a cake to help celebrate the occasion.

I still reflect on the adventure, and often when life gets stressful, I wish I was back on the river, camping on a sandbar surrounded by nothing but the sky and water. Unbelievably I still have sore tendons in my fingers, tan lines, and of course scars from my burns. I doubt they will ever leave me.

I am still in touch with the numerous people who helped us on our journey, and I will be eternally thankful for all the help they gave. On reflection they made the journey what it was.

I think the biggest thing I have learnt from the whole thing is about my level of mental toughness. To this day I have no idea how I managed to make myself get back in my kayak and carry-on day after day, how I got through the mind numbing 10-12 rigorous hours of paddling a day, how I survived cut off from the civilisation for days at a time, and how on earth I managed going weeks without having a shower! Joking apart, whilst on the Mississippi, and during my many 'low points', it often felt as though I had no mental toughness. All I wanted to do was give up and go home, but something kept me going. You may call it stubbornness, pride, or anything you want to, but I'm going with resilience and an extreme level of determination that I never really knew I had.

I still find it hard to summarise to people just what the trip was like (hopefully this book will help). I just know now that however hard life gets, if I can kayak while suffering from second degree burns, carry on going when everything seems impossible, and motivate myself to keep going when all my mind and body want to do is run away, I can do anything.

Anyway, I will end this here. Thank you for reading this book I hope you enjoyed it and maybe it has even inspired you to go out and have your own adventure (I take no responsibility for that).

At the point of closing our fundraising efforts we raised over £75,000 for the Theodora Children's Charity, which I still find incredible and overwhelming.

It wouldn't be sensible to say this will be the last book I ever write as already I am coming up with ideas of new challenges. I'm sure I will come up with something just as crazy and challenging as this one, but for now I'm off on a well-deserved holiday to the coast with my newly purchased Kayak…

Grace

Printed in Great Britain
by Amazon